REVELATIONS:

a collection of gay male
coming out stories

edited by
Wayne Curtis

Boston • Alyson Publications, Inc.

Typeset and printed in the United States of America.

Published as a trade paperback original
by Alyson Publications
40 Plympton Street
Boston, Mass. 02118.

Distributed in the U.K. by GMP Publishers,
PO Box 247, London, N15 6RW, England.

First U.S. edition: October, 1988

ISBN 1-55583-143-5

Revelations
production and design: Wayne Curtis
proofreading: Tina Portillo
printing: McNaughton & Gunn Lithographers

Contents

Introduction

"When did you come out?"

The question is inescapable. Every gay man has his story, and his friends and lovers will, sooner or later, ask him to tell it. It is our common bond with one another, uniting the different races, classes, educational backgrounds, and other groups that make up the gay community. Whether or not our lives have shared the same experiences, a coming out story stirs a powerful empathy in each of us, and brings to mind our own years of fear and pain.

The fear of exposure, of rejection, of an isolated life; the pain of lost families, lost self-esteem, lost love: few gay men have not let these influences cut their lives into fragments at one time or another. Modern society is a wilderness of prejudice, and even hatred, that consciously labors to suppress what it doesn't understand, or what it considers different and exotic. Coming out is not only a personal statement of worth and self-respect, it is a statement of dissent — a voice raised in defense of diversity and genuine democracy.

Yet for all the bonding together generated by the experience of coming out, it means vastly different things to different individuals. Each of the twenty-two stories in this collection offers a varying approach to the subject. Often it was the perspective, regardless of the degree of literary quality, that recommended a particular essay and assured it a place in this collection. I felt it was important for this book to reflect as much of the gay community as possible, including those voices that criticize it from within.

The twenty-two men whose lives make up this work vary widely in age and background. Some accepted, even as children, that they liked other boys in a way that made them different from most of their peers. Others fought that realization through years of marriage, children, and even grandchildren. Several discovered that coming out was only one barrier they faced; their ethnic background or physical condition was a source of discrimination even from their "brothers" in the gay community.

This diversity among the contributors guarantees a variety of definitions of coming out. To one it might mean learning to love and respect himself. To another, coming out is the feeling of freedom that accompanies walking down the street hand-in-hand with his lover. Each writer does share one important quality – the courage to see his life in print and to share his story with people he will never meet.

In many cases I felt that only minor editing was necessary on a particular story. Where more extensive changes or additions were required, I have worked closely with the author to preserve the integrity of his message. Most of these men freely gave their permission to publish their name and city. Others initially hesitated, but later gave their consent. A few felt that such openness would endanger themselves, their lovers, and their families: an asterisk indicates where a penname has been substituted for the author's own.

The day will come when the need for such precaution will vanish. But today, coming out and displaying gay pride is still a dangerous business. If this collection of essays can shore up a collapsing self-image somewhere, or share some hope in this dark wilderness of self-hatred, then its purpose will be accomplished. The day when we can all celebrate our identity will be one step closer.

Wayne Curtis
Boston, Mass.

REVELATIONS

Wilton Beggs
Dallas, Texas

Revelation

Even now I remember my awakening as if it were yesterday, each detail precise, undiminished by the passage of time. How could I forget the most important day of my youth?

It was late August, 1950. I was sixteen that summer, and in those days Pine Mill was a sluggish East Texas town, smaller, more insular than now, almost forty years later. Human activity that hot afternoon was minimal. Only a few people moved about the square.

The courthouse in the center of the square dominated our town. It was an architectural nightmare of Gothic arches, corner towers, and false battlements. Ancient trees shaded its lawns. Beneath the trees were slatted benches, empty that afternoon except for three old men. A statue of a Confederate veteran stood behind the bench where the old men sat.

I was looking out a window of Moore's Drugstore when I saw Martin Deaver come out of a courthouse door with his usual long-legged swagger. I was instantly alert: Martin's angry scowl could mean trouble. Pine Mill's tall, good-looking football hero, Martin had been my neighbor since I was born. The Deavers were respectable. Martin's father was a successful merchant and a deacon in the Southern Baptist Church.

The son, however, was no saint. Eleven months older than I and more muscular, a natural foe of anyone who read books, Martin had evidenced a brash, almost cheerful contempt toward me for as long as I could remember. My first black eye at the age of seven came from his fist. Over the years other bruises were tokens of his displeasure. I had never won a fight with him, and I considered him a mental throwback to the Neanderthals. Yet our proximity in a small town made us inevitable associates. My father, a carpenter, had built the Deaver family home, and I shared a number of friends with Martin. We were in no way chums, but neither were we absolute enemies.

He's mad and hunting for someone, I thought as I watched Martin stride across the lawn in my direction. His handsome head was cocked angrily; I could see his chest rise and fall. I breathed a quick prayer that he would stay out of the drugstore. I had no doubt Martin — if his mood were foul enough — could create a pointless scene just for the drama.

"All I need is that bum getting me fired," I muttered.

I had good reason to be apprehensive. There were seldom enough dollars in my family, and to earn spending money I was working in the store that summer for Mr. Shale Moore. An acrimonious widower who knew I needed the job very much, Mr. Moore would take pleasure in blaming me for any disturbance Martin might cause.

I grunted with loathing as I watched Martin spit amber juice on the lawn. Forbidden cigarettes by the school football coach, Martin and some of his teammates had recently begun chewing tobacco. I thought it a disgusting vice, though several of the boys involved were among the more desirable young men in town.

My perception of my schoolmates' attractiveness I kept strictly private. Although at sixteen I knew where my sexual preference lay, I had found no way to act upon it. In my mind I was a pariah already, a latter-day brother of the biblical degenerates who had caused the destruction of Sodom.

Like most of my generation, I was unaware that there were,

somewhere, people of my kind about whom I could feel pride. My horizon had never encompassed a gay writer, actor, or artist. I could not have imagined a gay lifestyle of any type. For me the millenniums of gay history, our enviable contribution to Western culture, our very *being*, was nonexistent. I had never heard of a homosexual publication, nor seen a motion picture that touched in any recognizable manner on the subject. No one had hinted to me that there might actually be organizations of gay people in my world. In truth, I did not know the word "gay" meant anything other than "merry." And that summer I was not merry.

At sixteen, though the son of loving and well-intentioned parents, I felt increasingly alone, racked by emotions I was sure no one of any worth had ever experienced. I thought myself unique in the worst sense of the word, and lived in real fear that Martin or someone of his caliber would discover my shameful secret. Should that happen, I could not fathom how I would continue my life.

As Martin was gathering the saliva in his mouth for another amber stream, I saw a girl walk past the bench where the three elderly men were sitting. Martin showed immediate interest in her. Glaring, his frown more pronounced than before, he stepped forward into a pool of sunlight. The newcomer did not notice him. Martin was almost hidden from her by the statue. She hurried on unheedingly, heels clicking on sun-dappled pavement.

Martin wore a look of incredulous outrage as his eyes followed the girl. A moment passed, then I watched him turn and head toward a telephone booth beside a courthouse door. The girl hurried on, and did not glance around until she reached the corner of the square. By this time Martin was inside the booth, his back to her.

On the shaded bench the three old men mumbled together and punched one another with sharp elbows. In a town where everyone knew his neighbor, and many were kin, such a flamboyant stranger was bound to cause comment.

The girl — for Pine Mill — was spectacular. Her figure was slender but feminine, her face aristocratic with a classic Greek nose and great brown eyes. Her hair was a dark auburn that fell below her shoulders. Rather tall, she held herself well, and each movement flowed into the next. Her red dress was garish, with plunging neck and fringed hem. Out-sized jewelry gave her a tawdry appearance belied by the patrician face. In one hand she clutched a cardboard suitcase. I guessed her to be about twenty.

She waited for an automobile to pass, then started across the brick street just as Martin left the phone booth and quickly followed her. The girl pulled the drugstore door open and almost ran inside. The swirling blades of the ceiling fans stirred her hair as she let the door swing to with a spanking noise. Seeing the store had no customers, she gave me a hesitant glance. I realized she was frightened. Up close I saw her makeup had been applied in the lustrous fashion an actress might use. This emphasized even more the odd impression of bluff and innocence.

"Can I help you?" I remember saying inanely.

As she approached me I sensed something exotically knowable about the girl, but my mind could not identify it. I stepped behind the counter of the soda fountain and waited. She regarded me with a wary half-smile.

"I don't know why I did this," she whispered. "I'm scared silly. You don't recognize me?"

The words were breathless. Nonplussed, I shook my head. She gave a laugh. Nearly my height, she stared at me apprehensively for several seconds.

"Maybe you know my kinfolks," she said at last, her voice husky. "The Askews?"

"The Southern Baptist preacher?" I began to understand why she seemed familiar. "You *do* favor his daughter. Betty's the prettiest girl in Pine Mill."

She hesitated. "Well, Betty's my cousin."

She moved forward in a self-conscious manner that struck me as slightly incongruous, suddenly rather clumsy. She pointed to a time chart on the wall behind me.

"I need a bus ticket. I have to get out of here!"

Like many small East Texas towns even today, Pine Mill had no genuine bus station. Buses pulled off the highway and stopped on the square. Passengers arrived at and departed from the sidewalk in front of the drugstore.

I ran a finger down the list of cities. "Where to?"

"The first bus out," she said flatly. I must have shown my perplexity, for she bit her lip and forced an unconvincing smile. "The bus to Dallas," she said, flushing.

Her nervousness was contagious. I stared at her with wonder, realizing how close she was to panic.

"What's wrong?" Not knowing why, I felt somehow involved. "Is Martin Deaver bothering you?"

She glared at me, the color draining from her cheeks. Her rather large hands were clenched. There was no sound except the creaking of the ceiling fans.

"Have you seen Martin?" she asked hoarsely.

Before I could speak we heard the slap of the drugstore door. The girl winced, but did not turn as the thump of Martin's boots filled the room. I drew back from the counter involuntarily, for his face was a mask of rage.

The girl stood motionless as the footsteps came closer. Much taller than she was, Martin halted directly behind her. The rasp of his breathing was ominous. No one spoke. She stared ahead, at me, blank-faced, as if blocking out his presence.

He hit her, hard. The blow knocked her upon the counter. Her suitcase slipped from her hand, the clasps breaking open, male shirts and trousers spilling out. I was paralyzed by shock. Again Martin struck her, and she fell to the floor. An earring skidded over the tiles until it hit a wall and shattered. The girl lay inertly, face down, unprotesting.

Coming to my senses, I jumped over the counter and grabbed Martin's arm. "You'll hurt her bad!" I said in horror.

Martin's blue eyes were points of flame. His handsome face was slack-jawed, hideous with a passion I could not read. He jerked in frustration as I fought to keep him from the girl.

"Stay out of this, fool," he said roughly. I clung to him to keep from being hurled aside. "You're too stupid to understand!"

The door at the rear of the room sprang open. Shale Moore, my employer, came running across the long expanse. Shale, in those days, was a fat, graceless old person with frowzy white hair and the disposition of a shrew. Seeing his wide-eyed indignation, I was sure my employment would soon be terminated. He rushed up to us and made ineffectual shushing motions with knobby hands.

"Goddamn bastards!" he yelled, for Shale was profane as most people in that era were not, and excessively ill-tempered. "Take your fighting outside!"

Shale was about to make further demands when he became aware of the girl. His eyes were bulging wider as Shale advanced and nudged her with his foot. The girl groaned and sat up. She leaned back against the counter painfully. A trickle of blood ran down her cheek from a superficial cut on the temple. The girl glowered at Martin, her fear apparently under control.

"Who's *that*?" said Shale. His wrinkled countenance was swathed in resentment. "What y'all been doing in my store?"

Martin did not answer. His eyes were locked with the girl's in an unreadable duel. Guarding myself watchfully, I loosened my grip on his arms and stepped back. He paid me no attention.

"Who is this woman?" Shale said stridently. "What's wrong with the bitch?"

"Don't y'all know Cary Askew?" Martin said with a sneer. "Take a good look."

His shirt damp with perspiration, Martin walked over to the girl and pulled at her hair. I was dumbfounded when the hair gave way and I saw Martin clutching a long auburn wig in his hand. Beneath the wig was the close-cropped blond head of a boy. The boy had a painted face and wore a gaudy red dress — and was, beyond any doubt, Cary Askew, Betty Askew's sixteen-year-old brother.

"What the *hell*?" said Shale Moore. "She's a fellow!"

I was gaping, unable to move. If a meteor had crashed through the ceiling I could not have been more astonished. I knew Cary Askew to be a quiet, diffident boy who made excellent grades in school and was something of a star during baseball season. He was my friend. I had "run" with him most of my life. Nothing in our past had prepared me for this.

"A *dress*," said Shale disbelievingly. "And stuffed tits! One of Preacher Askew's kids!"

Although I did not speak, I could not help sharing Shale's dismay. The situation was too bizarre for my limited experience. True to my upbringing, I had not penetrated Cary's disguise — mainly because it had never occurred to me that a man of our town could dress as a woman.

"A goddamn painted boy!" said Shale, terribly offended. "In that wig he looked like a woman ten years older!"

Martin wiped his mouth grimly. "He's sick, Mr. Moore. His sister told me about him a year ago. That's Betty's stage outfit he's got on."

"He must be nuts," said Shale. "I never heard of such a thing!"

Looking at Cary I remembered Betty Askew's costume for the high school play that previous May. She had portrayed a dance-hall wench reformed by a noble rustic. Though a "moral" comedy, the play had been thought too daring by some in the community, and the Reverend Askew — a man of stern beliefs — had apologized later to his congregation for allowing his daughter's participation. The dress Cary had on, complete with jewelry, was Pine Mill's version of what a wanton should wear.

"I've been going with Betty since the tenth grade," Martin told Shale confidentially. "Brother Askew knows his son's crazy. When I saw that dress out there on the square, I phoned Betty, and she said both Cary *and* it were missing."

"Get that scum out of here," Shale snapped. He darted a sharp glance at the front window. "What if somebody sees him? What would folks say? The Askews were my late wife's cousins. This is pure shit!"

Shale made an imperious gesture to me, and I began shoving clothes back into Cary's suitcase. I felt numb, dazed by conflicting emotions, as I snapped the clasps and handed the suitcase to him. Digging into a pocket, I gave Cary my handkerchief to wipe the blood from his cheek.

"They think I'm crazy, so why not *be*?" he said. His voice was shaking, but altogether masculine as he looked at me squarely. "Why not give them a show?"

I felt myself turn crimson. In his mien was an implication of intimacy that was chilling. I was as embarrassed as if he had stripped me naked. I realized he *knew*.

"I'm not the only one in this town who's crazy," he said.

I drew back, appalled. Against my will I recalled with shamed vividness the nights Cary and I had spent together as buddies during the past year. Had I been so obvious, stealing my guilt-ridden glances as we undressed for bed? Had he, as I, experienced the confused and desperate needs I had suppressed?

"Take him in back," Shale said with disgust. "Wash the paint off and get him in shirt and pants. I'll call his daddy to come fetch him." He snorted. "Askew will *kill* the little punk."

Cary's face went white beneath the makeup. He got to his feet unsteadily.

"Let me alone," he said to Martin. "Martin, don't make things any worse."

"I can make it any way I want it, sonny." Martin tossed the wig behind the counter, grabbed Cary's wrist, and pulled him away. "Your pop expects me to whip you into a regular person."

I heard this with skepticism. Although Martin had dated Betty Askew for a couple of years, and his father was a leader in their church, I was sure Brother Askew disapproved of Martin, anyway. Martin's reputation extended beyond Pine Mill. Several escapades with wilder girls of the county, plus a rumor that he had fathered a baby, had made Martin a dubious candidate for marriage to a strict minister's daughter. But Betty was smitten. Despite his blatant unfaithfulness I knew Betty dated no one but him, and I thought it possible *she* had asked Martin to ride herd on her brother.

"I'll cure you yet, sissy," Martin taunted as he towed Cary along. He shook his fist in the smaller boy's face. "Here's the medicine for queers."

At this threat Cary gave such a hooting, cynical laugh that I jumped. "Hypocrite!" he said.

Cary's hysterical laughter was cut off as Martin slapped him. Martin shoved him through the door. It closed, and Shale and I were left with the silence of the room broken only by a murmur of ceiling fans.

"Holy Brother Askew thought my wife lowered herself marrying me," Shale chuckled. He hitched up his baggy trousers and walked to the telephone behind the counter. "I'll make that pious son-of-a-bitch squirm."

I glanced about me in a daze. Mere minutes had passed since I had noticed Martin across the street. The afternoon sun had not moved perceptibly. Through the window I could still see the three old men sitting on their bench.

"Martin was mad before he spotted Cary," I said. "It was like he was already looking for him, Mr. Moore."

Taking the telephone receiver from its cradle, Shale fixed me with his gimlet stare. "Worry about *me* being mad, boy. If you want to keep working here, forget this. It's bad for business. The damn Askews are my meat."

I regarded the old man with open dislike. "Cary's my friend," I said shortly. "I wouldn't rat on a friend."

Shale's thin cackle was laden with innuendo. "I'll bet you wouldn't, sweetums." His face crinkled in scorn. "Anybody into that sort of shit is better off dead."

I don't think I have ever hated anyone so much as I did Shale Moore at that moment. It is the earliest encounters with heterosexual arrogance that hurt you the most.

"Quit gawking," Shale said gruffly. "I'll tell his pa to drive down the alley. I don't want my customers exposed to this crap. You help Martin get that queer into some decent clothes." His large-knuckled fingers began dialing the telephone. "Y'all have your *friend* ready when the preacher gets here."

Seething with resentment at his mocking tone, I went to the rear of the store. My hand was on the doorknob before the realization struck me that I was no longer alone in Pine Mill. The force of the notion was numbing.

Cary is too, I remember thinking to myself with awe. A freak like me! I had been floundering for so long with my forbidden desires, convinced no one else in the universe had my affliction — and now, without warning, I had discovered Cary Askew was a monster, also. The initial glimmering that someone in Pine Mill shared my secret was the closest I think I ever came to heaven.

I was shaking as I went into the darkened hallway and shut the door behind me. Water splashed in the restroom to my right. I moved forward quietly, then stopped for a while, gathering my confused thoughts. Minutes passed before voices became audible. Neither Martin nor Cary had yet detected my presence.

"Keep away from me, Martin," I heard Cary say, low. "I hate you."

I leaned against the wall, hardly breathing. I was so weak my knees threatened to buckle. Abruptly I guessed why Martin had been so upset even before he spied Cary on the courthouse lawn.

"You were with Andy Newcomb last night," Martin was saying furiously. "You were in Andy's car!"

The rank, sexual jealousy was unmistakable. In the dimness of the hall I shook my head like a prizefighter who has sustained a violent blow. Andy Newcomb was a married man in his mid-twenties, the son of Pine Mill's mayor. At that moment I began to suspect dimensions to my restricted world I had never dreamed.

"If you don't leave me alone I'll tell them everything," Cary said hoarsely. "Daddy will beat me to a pulp, anyway." He paused, while the noise of running water diminished. "How'd you like Betty to know?"

There was a quick, keen report, and I knew Martin had hit Cary again. I clenched my fists, longing to harm Martin in any way I could.

"You filthy pansy," Martin spat. "I'm trying to help you!"

"Sure," said Cary bitterly. "That's why you can't stand me to even talk to another guy."

Before Martin could strike Cary again I slammed the wall with my elbow. The water shut off, and I could sense them listening.

"You're a coward, Martin," Cary said softly into the silence. "At least I'm honest with myself."

The door banged open, and Martin was scowling at me, the light of the restroom flooding around him. I thought for a moment he would attack me, for his manner was that of a cornered animal. With a baleful curse he swung and went out into the alley. I heard his footsteps hurrying away.

It was some time before I could summon enough courage to walk to the restroom door. When I moved into the light Cary was standing beside the wash basin, his wounded eyes level with mine. He had removed the makeup and jewelry, and was clothed in jeans and a plaid shirt. While I watched he pushed his feet into a pair of scuffed loafers. The red dress and padded bra lay crumpled beside the open suitcase. He looked very vulnerable but not at all feminine.

"I figured it was you," he said. "I've sure made a mess, haven't I? Damn, I don't even *want* to be a girl."

His face was pale and scared. I put out my hand. He gripped it tightly.

"I don't understand," I remember saying, trying to puzzle it out. "Why'd you dress up like that?"

"Honest, I don't really know." He managed a self-deprecating smile, and I recall thinking him the bravest, most beautiful boy I had ever seen. "Maybe to show them I'm as bad as they think, because it's the stuff they accuse me of." He shrugged. "Maybe just to show Daddy I'm not afraid of his rotten Hell."

I caught my breath, and the dam burst: "Well, I don't care if I go there, either!"

With a grateful sigh I will never forget, Cary put his arms around me. "I've tried to tell you a dozen times this year," he said. I remember his kissing me then, and the frantic way my heart pounded against my chest as if it would burst. "I *knew* you were like me."

"At least your dad won't be with us in Hell," I said.

He chuckled and held me tighter. "A place like that can't be all bad, can it?"

I think those minutes with Cary Askew, in Pine Mill the summer I was sixteen, must have been the happiest of my life.

Dan Restid

Ellwood City, Pennsylvania

Ending the Charade

I knew the moment that I walked into the house on that crisp evening in January of 1984 that something was seriously wrong. One need not be married long to be able to sense your spouse's moods, and the vibrations this evening indicated serious trouble indeed. I kicked off my snow-covered shoes in the hallway and made my way toward the bedroom, hoping along the way that the source of my wife's aloofness was not what I was suspecting.

When I entered the bedroom, however, I discovered that my fears were well founded, because a suitcase lay open on the bed just aching to be packed.

"What's that out for?" I asked, feigning amusement. "Are you planning a trip?"

"You and I have something serious to discuss," came the cool reply.

My wife had been cleaning that afternoon and discovered a gay magazine that I thought had been well concealed.

"I was so sick when I found this," she said tearfully. "I think you owe me an explanation."

I offered the only consolation that my shock would allow: "Well, they say that you can take the boy out of the country, but you can't take the country out of the boy."

That was the beginning of the end of my marriage.

I can't remember a time that I was not gay. Even when I was tender in years and unable to comprehend the complexities of relationships and the mechanics of sexual expression, my sexual orientation seemed to be an integral part of my nature. Now, I can understand why I developed strong affections for other little boys and why playing doctor with them was so exciting.

In high school, I became an avid bun watcher and the scenery in the shower room inspired sexual fantasies which enhanced the pleasure of my adolescent masturbation. I had only one partner during these years of sexual awakening because I was sheltered, ignorant about the effective methods of seduction, and fearful of being caught and embarrassed. I ignored several sexual come-ons in high school because I was too naive to recognize them for what they were.

Several months after graduating in 1969, I found myself on the threshold of an emotional disorder. Panic attacks: frightening sensations caused by a chemical imbalance in the brain. In 1974, I foolishly convinced myself that these attacks were God's way of punishing me for being gay and ignoring the biblical advice that there was no place in God's kingdom for "men who lie with men." So in November of 1975, I re-dedicated myself as a Jehovah's Witness, a cult that I was raised with but despised during my youth, hoping that piety would put an end to my emotional discomfort. I soon married a member of this sect, knowing that I was not willing to satisfy her physical needs and falsely believing that marriage and religion would make me straight.

There were few people in Ellwood City, Pennsylvania, in those days who knew that I was gay, but enough to cause trouble for my new wife and me if they were so inclined. One week after the wedding, therefore, I told my bride about my past; I felt she would rather hear it from me than someone else.

"Promise me something," she said. "Just don't ever mention this again."

And it never was — until that evening in 1984 when she confronted me with the magazine. But throughout the seven years in between, I could feel the tension permeating the air whenever homosexuality was mentioned on television or by unsuspecting friends.

The security of my marriage was one excuse for remaining closeted. I was also hindered by the knowledge that if I came out I would be shunned by the members of this strict religious order, including a number of family members. But the real obstacle was me — me with my morbid fear of failure and my preoccupation with the uncertainty of success. I preferred to remain in the misery of my present circumstances rather than risk coming out and finding myself in more desperate ones. Because of this reluctance, I had no peace of mind and caused untold anguish for myself and others.

Being a Jehovah's Witness was a farce. I hated adhering to all the rigid demands of the Watchtower Society, the governing organization of the worldwide sect. But I gloried in the acceptance of others, particularly my mother. Sexual activity with my wife was simply obligatory; my true longing was to be free to express myself sexually in the manner that was natural for me. Shortly before my son was born, my panic attacks were so intense that I had to quit a new job on the very first day. I then realized that I needed professional help, regardless of my faith's negative view of psychiatry. My analyst suggested that I seek the services of the Persad Center, a Pittsburgh counseling service for sexual minorities. I declined, fearful that it would intensify my desires and endanger my relationships. By 1984, I was unable to keep up the charade. I gradually discontinued all religious activities and completely severed God from my life. Praying and reading the Bible seemed futile for someone like me.

In the spring of 1985, the panic attacks were so severe that I was plotting my suicide. The doctors arranged for hospitalization in a psychiatric ward. The evening before being admitted, I became engulfed with a feeling that I would never recover and slumped into an unequaled depression. Turning my face to the wall, I laid everything on God's shoulders, telling Him that I could not honestly serve Him as a Jehovah's Witness or as one of a moral majority who denounced homosexuals, but just as me — just as I am.

The depression evaporated; my improvement was gradual and steady. God fortified me for the significant changes that were to take place in my life. I attended a consciousness-raising group at Persad Center in Pittsburgh. I had my spirituality renewed through reading gay literature with a religious slant by authors like Maury Johnston and Rev. Sylvia Pennington. I discovered that gays have a place in God's heart, and many have been saved and experienced the baptism of the Holy Spirit. They have, like me, reclaimed their sense of self-worth.

In December of 1985, I voluntarily dissolved my bond with the Watchtower organization and was divorced in the spring of 1986. Although it has meant complete alienation from family and friends, I now live a happy, fulfilling and stimulating life, and I am making many new friends in the gay community.

Larry Duplechan
Los Angeles, California

Birthday Present:
a reminiscence

Among the "Acknowledgements" at the beginning of my second novel, *Blackbird*, is one that reads: "Larry R., for the best eighteenth birthday present a kid ever got." This is the story of that present.

It was Saturday, December 30, 1974. Gerald R. Ford was president. "Lucy in the Sky With Diamonds" by Elton John was number one with a bullet on the *Billboard* pop charts. It was the best of times. It was the worst of times. It was my eighteenth birthday. I was at work.

I was just another eighteen-year-old black gay college freshman at U.C.L.A., helping to meet the high cost of my higher education by working part-time at the McDonald's in Westwood Village (in those days a bustling college town; in these days one of the world's largest shopping malls, with a major university quite inexplicably attached to it, like an appendix). Bachelor's degrees were expensive, even then.

I worked the grill, flipping Big Macs, frying fries, secretly sampling dill pickle slices. I bore the scars of a thousand grease burns from my wrists to my armpits; and on those days when I'd dash from school down Westwood Boulevard to the Golden Arches to put in a couple of quick hours between classes, I invariably returned to campus with ketchup behind my ears, smelling mighty like a Quarter Pounder with cheese.

More than once the store manager — a scruffy walrus of a man named Bill with a penchant for loud, fat neckties and too much Brut aftershave — had offered me a cashier gig, which would have afforded me a bit more money and far fewer grease burns. I'd refused. Not because I enjoyed working the grill (Would a snowman enjoy a summer in Miami?) but because even though, as an English Lit major, I had read *Beowulf* and understood most of it, and could recite from memory the first several stanzas of the Prologue to the *Canterbury Tales* in a better than average Middle-English accent; and despite an embarrassingly high I.Q., a current 3.75 grade point average, and a lightning wit; I could not make change. Not at gunpoint. Still can't.

Anyway — on that Saturday afternoon some forty-eight hours shy of 1975, I was lowering a basket of frozen apple pies into a bubbling deep fat vat; only half-cognizant of the two or three other grill workers chattering away in Spanish (I was the only person on the grill team born north of the Mexican border) when I was startled by a surreptitious tickle to my lower rib cage. I turned quickly and looked into the grinning face of our district manager, Robert. (Actually, Robert was not his real name. His real name was Larry. And my name is Larry. And two guys named Larry in one small story could get a trifle confusing. So we'll call him Robert, okay?)

Robert was thirty years old — I'd asked. He had butch-cut blond hair and pale blue eyes and an infectiously boyish grin that never failed to make me want to bite my lip. It was a Mickey-Rooney-as-Andy-Hardy grin crossed with what I would years later term the *Mandate* centerfold fuck-you grin.

"Hey, big Larry," Robert said in his testosterone-laced bedroom-basso voice. Robert liked to call me "big Larry" — a small joke, as I've never been what you'd call a large person. He tossed me another grin.

I saw his grin, and raised him a giggle and a quick, breathy "Hi."

"So what's new?" Robert pretended to adjust the oversized

collar of my oversized blue work smock. He stood so close I could smell his cologne, even over the all-pervasive smell of junk food.

"Today's my birthday," I said. "I'm eighteen today." I had to look up a little to meet Robert's eyes. We were really just about the same height; but I was wearing Hush Puppies, and Robert was wearing shoes with two-inch heels. Very cool shoes in 1974. He was also wearing a beige doubleknit suit — very cool threads in 1974 — and his trim, small-waisted body did quite well by it.

"Well," Robert said, "happy birthday."

"So what are you going to give me?" I smiled what I hoped was a playfully seductive smile.

Robert paused a moment, and grinned another one of those grins.

"Not to worry," he said finally. "We'll think of something."

And he walked away, his high shoes clicking against the greasy floor. I watched his well-shouldered beige doubleknit back moving away, and I wondered if Robert was going to give me what I wanted for my birthday.

I suppose now is as good a point as any to mention that as of the afternoon of my eighteenth birthday, I was a virgin. Purer than Ivory soap; untouched as the parsley garnish on a T-bone steak.

Which is not to say I hadn't known what I wanted for years. Because, believe me, I'd known. I'd acknowledged myself as gay at around the age of thirteen. I read the chapter on homosexuality in *Everything You've Always Wanted to Know About Sex*, and thought: *yep, that's me alrighty*. And I'd been falling madly, passionately, head-over-tuchus in love with a veritable parade of boys since Mike McCarthy unwittingly stole my twelve-year-old heart in the seventh grade. But as of that Saturday afternoon of December 30, 1974 — not counting masturbation (and let's just say I jerked off quite a lot and leave it at that) — I had never had sex.

Which is not to say I didn't really want to, because believe me, I really wanted to. It wasn't as if I'd had no offers, because in the four months or so since I'd left home for college, I'd had my share. I attended the Gay Students Union meetings at school every Tuesday night, quite undiscouraged by the fact that at the first meeting I'd attended, in a simple white t-shirt and 501s ensemble, I was almost immediately mistaken for a lesbian. *By* a lesbian. I hadn't started lifting weights yet.

Still, over several weeks' worth of meetings, I'd had offers. I was asked home by a smallish (but not entirely unattractive) bush-league poet wearing wire-rimmed eyeglasses with only one lens. I was approached by an overweight black man in his mid-fifties. (Now I don't want to get into a big age thing here, but my *father* was in his late forties at this point, okay?) A willowy blond who called himself Golden, in a pale pink shirt and about a hundred silver bracelets, informed me (in a lisp you could water your ficus with) that he was strongly attracted to the innate savagery of the black male; and I might have obliged him with whatever savagery I could muster — he was very pretty, after all — if it wasn't that I've always liked my men to be just a little more, well, manly. I was propositioned by a tall, dark, handsome Greek with shoulder-length hair, who invited me to spend the evening with him, his girlfriend, and a large jar of Miracle Whip. Not exactly how I'd envisioned my first time, y'know?

So, one thing and another, I was still a virgin. I mean, I'd waited this long, so why not hold out for someone halfway decent, right?

Then there was Robert. Good-looking and sexy and just old enough — a man of some experience, more than likely. And he liked me, this much was certain. Who better to relieve me of the ever more cumbersome burden of my virginity? Provided he was gay, of course, which I wasn't exactly sure of yet. I mean, how could I be sure? Sure, he smiled at me a lot, and winked at me. And tickled me. And patted my ass. Okay, I was pretty sure.

There was the time Robert found me in the walk-in refrigerator, taking inventory of frozen hamburger patties. Robert peeked in and said, "Boy, you could really freeze your balls off in there." Big pause while he lifted one golden eyebrow and grinned for me. "And we certainly wouldn't want *that*!"

There was the time Robert spotted me stacking brownies onto a big plastic platter and walked over to me, stood just close enough to make my skin prickle, and whispered into my ear, "Hello, little brownie."

And then of course, there was the historic Cut Finger Incident.

Two or three weeks before my birthday, after several weeks of smiles and tickles and winky-winky with Robert, I'd pulled the not exactly exciting task of refilling non-food inventory: which consisted mostly of slicing open large corrugated cardboard cartons of various supplies (little packets of ketchup, boxes of coffee stirrers, those little containers your french fries come in — that sort of thing), and stacking these supplies on the shelves in the stock room. Fabulous, right?

So anyway, I'm upstairs in the stock room, slicing open these big boxes of, say, Filet-O-Fish sandwich wrappers with an Exacto knife, probably singing to myself (maybe "Lucy in the Sky With Diamonds"), when who should appear at the top of the staircase but Robert. Not having heard anyone come up the stairs, and momentarily startled by the sudden appearance of anybody (let alone Robert), my knife-wielding right hand slipped, slicing a very impressive gash in my left index finger. Very showy, lots of blood. Not very deep, though.

Now, I'm not real good with blood. My own, that is. Not that I get hysterical or anything. On the contrary: I tend to watch myself bleed with a sort of calm fascination, until I go into shock. So I'm just standing there, watching my finger spurt blood all over these Filet-O-Fish sandwich wrappers, when Robert says, "Dr. Robert to the rescue!"

He moved quickly to the first aid kit mounted on a nearby wall (the stock room was probably the scene of many an Exacto knife injury); and before I even had time to go into shock, Robert had blotted my blood with a cotton ball, spritzed my finger with Bactine, and wrapped it in a large ouchless Curad.

We just stood there for a moment: Robert holding my injured hand up between our faces, me staring past my wound and into Robert's blue eyes.

"You gonna be all right?" he asked.

I nodded.

"You want me to kiss it and make it all better?"

I nodded vigorously.

And you know what? The man actually kissed my finger. That was when I became — well — pretty sure Robert liked me. I mean really *liked* me.

So back to my birthday:

Shortly after I'd announced my birthday to Robert, he came

walking back through the grill area. He stopped directly behind me where I stood shooting Big Mac sauce onto buns with a big sauce gun.

"Eighteen, huh?" he said to the back of my head.

"Yep."

"Hm. Street legal."

Street legal? Robert moved in a little closer.

"How about I give you a ride home after work today?" Robert whispered into the nape of my neck, making every hair on my body stand at attention.

"Okay."

For the remainder of my shift, I was largely incapable of work. I would have been hard pressed to recognize a hamburger in a room full of objects. A ride home. This, I thought to myself, was It.

And then things really start to blur. I, who pride myself on my astounding memory for detail, for being able to recall large swaths of my life with the crispness and clarity of a fine motion picture; I find I only remember the next hour or so in bits and pieces, like those smeared, blurry black-and-white photographs we used to take with Polaroid "Swinger" cameras.

I remember Robert steering me out the back door of the store, calling "Lunch!" over his shoulder to whomever, and my heart pounding like a jackhammer. I remember he drove me home in a white Corvette with red leather upholstery. I remember he stopped at a liquor store and bought a bottle of creme de Cassis and a large bag of Doritos. I remember he grabbed my thigh between gear-shiftings, and my dick got so hard so fast I nearly blacked out.

We sat in the miniscule living area of the single apartment I shared with the sort of nonentity roommate that college life seems to inflict upon the best of us. Luckily, he worked Saturdays, too. And we ate tortilla chips and drank Cassis (which, to tell the truth, I don't much like), and we talked about . . . something. Again, blur. But needless to say, you could have sliced, diced, crinkle-cut, and julienned the sexual tension in the room.

At one point, I got up to refill our glasses in the kitchen. I was standing at the kitchen counter, pouring the stuff; and when I turned around, a full glass in each hand, there was Robert. Right there where I'd turned, so we were practically nose to nose. And I went to hand Robert his glass, but he didn't take it. So I'm just standing there like a schmuck, holding a Cassis on the rocks in each hand, and just barely breathing, when Robert kissed me. Softly. Sweetly. On my lips.

I'd been waiting all my life for that kiss. After all the years of wanting it, wishing for it, fantasizing about it, I'd finally been kissed by a man. And there was more where that came from. Robert kissed me again, a little more insistently this time, playing his tongue along my upper lip. It was at that point that I asked in an understandably breathy tone if I could put the glasses down. Robert laughed and took the drinks from my hands, and put them on the counter behind me.

My hands freed, I wrapped my arms around Robert, and we kissed. Robert kissed my face and eyelids and throat, dallied his tongue-tip in both my ears, making me gasp. I touched him everywhere I could reach, stroked his prickly short-short hair, kneaded big handfuls of his beige doubleknit behind, and ate up Robert's sweet kisses like candy. They *were* like candy: good and plenty.

I sighed aloud as Robert unbuttoned my shirt and kissed his way down to my nipples, and sucked first one, then the other, to puckered erection. I was so full of the smell and taste and feel of this sweet hot blue-eyed man, not to mention the immediate discovery of the nipples as an erogenous zone (nobody ever told me your chest could feel quite that good), that Robert managed to have my Levis unbuttoned and my dick out of my pants and waving him hello before I'd even noticed. Robert stepped back from me for a moment and looked at me: shirt open, pants down around my knees, leaning against my kitchen counter. He smiled a long, slow smile and said, "Beautiful."

Then he took me by the erect penis and led me (walking rather like a geisha girl, what with my pants down to my knees) to my bed.

What happened next is the stuff of the sort of story usually found between photographs of naked boys with homemade tattoos on their arms, in those dog-eared magazines you keep under the bed next to the Hot Lube, the Trojans, and that little leather whatchacallit. And this isn't one of those stories. So let's just say that, of the milestones in a young man's life — his first car, his first date, that sort of thing — few things, perhaps nothing compares with a boy's first blow job. At least, so it was for me.

It wasn't until Robert had finished, and I looked up to see him standing next to my bed, grinning that grin of his, that I realized he'd never removed a stitch of clothing. There I lay, sprawled, spent, and quite altogether naked on the bed; and there stood Robert, beige doubleknit suit still very much in evidence. I was thinking of mentioning this fact when Robert said, "Hey, you."

"Hey what?" I said.

And Robert sang, softly and not quite in tune: "Happy birthday to you/Happy birthday to you/Happy birthday big Larry—"

He stopped singing, wiggled an eyebrow at me and said, "And I *do* mean *big*!" Then he climbed back onto the bed, clothes and all, and hugged me a big, warm hug and kissed my lips, and whispered, "See you later, you little sexpot."

Then he climbed off me and off the bed, tiptoed out of the apartment, and was gone. Leaving me feeling about as good as California law will allow, touching my body where Robert had touched it, and singing softly to myself, "Happy birthday to me..."

Robert and I had sex a few times after that — once in the upstairs banquet room at McDonald's; on a table, no less. (Oh, what that man could do with mayonnaise!) But it was just fun and games — I couldn't even *pretend* to be in love with Robert; and even at eighteen I knew I wanted to be in love. So it just sort of petered out after a while. And within a year, I *was* in love. (But that's another story.)

Still, I'll never forget Robert — Larry R., that is. Or the present he gave me: my very first sexual experience — one that I'll always remember fondly. So, whether or not he ever sees the "Acknowledgements" to my second novel; whether he still remembers me or forgot me five minutes after our last tryst — I do hope he's well. And very happy. I honestly do.

Thomas Frasier
Baltimore, Maryland

Coming to Terms

Every Tuesday I usually have lunch with an old friend. More often than not, we talk about our respective childhoods. While we rarely talk about sex, I was not especially surprised one Tuesday when she asked me when I first realized I was gay.

"*Very* early," I answered. I wasn't sure when, exactly. It seemed like I always knew it, even before I knew what 'it' was.

"Did you ever feel that there was something wrong with you because you were gay?"

"No," I replied.

"You didn't feel any guilt?" she persisted.

"No."

"Really?" she asked suspiciously.

"Really," I replied, "I honestly never did."

"How wonderful!" she exclaimed.

Had my parents overlooked something while I was growing up? That seemed highly unlikely. *How* then?

I was born in a small town in the Upper Peninsula of Michigan, and raised there between the start of World War II and the end of the Korean War. If my friend at lunch was the determined survivor of a strict, upper middle-class upbringing in a prosperous Mid-Atlantic port city, then I was equally hard-pressed as a second generation gay descendant of steerage-class immigrants, who for some inexplicable reason were attracted to one of the most remote, sparsely settled areas of the Great Lakes region.

That part of the country has a long history of absorbing immigrants, beginning with the fur-traders when the area was still French. In the nineteenth century, Scandinavians and Poles came over to work in the woods, or in the iron and copper mines beside the Cornish, who arrived when the tin mines began closing in their region of England. There was also a small, clannish enclave of Greek restauranteurs, and one of Jewish merchants. Only the Finns continued to speak their native language after World War II, but even those of us who grew up speaking only English spoke it with a distinctive accent influenced by all these peoples.

The interaction of these ethnic groups was actually quite amicable, and surprisingly tolerant. In spite of some often wildly individualistic personalities, most everyone seemed reasonably flexible in forging a common life in spite of their differences. But not all differences were tolerated.

From time to time, men who lived in my hometown would leave quietly — for no apparent reason. But a lot of people were leaving. After World War II the area's economy started going downhill, and there were far more serious things for everyone to think about than their neighbor's sex life. The Upper Peninsula's biggest export was fast becoming something far more valuable than the gleanings from its war-depleted forests, or its copper and iron deposits — it was losing its people, including many gay men within the more visible exodus of straights.

The word homosexual was never used by my parents when I was growing up. When I was little, I was told not to accept candy from grown men. When I was in sixth grade, and three teenage boys gave me a ride home one day, my father said not to accept rides from them again. In both cases, no explanation was given. People didn't talk much about sex in the late forties and early fifties, or tell someone about to enter puberty any more than absolutely necessary — unless they caught you at it!

While it's hard to keep much of anything secret in a small town, that doesn't keep very many people from doing what they want to do. One day my Aunt Ann used a word I didn't know. She had been talking about Rita, a "maiden lady" who wore her prematurely grey hair cut in a boyish bob, and was a staunch member of the Methodist Church, which at the time was attracting a large following among the town's women. I don't remember now what the word was, but I do remember asking her what it meant.

Aunt Ann hesitated a moment before she answered, then she smiled, and replied, *"Rita likes to kiss other women the way most women like to kiss men."* I had seen women kiss each other, but till then it had never occurred to me that they might kiss *the same way* men and women were supposed to. If two women could do that, then two men could do it, too! And *that* possibility excited me very much, even then — especially when I thought of some of my older sister's boyfriends.

By the time my peer group began to enter puberty, we knew all the "dirty" words. We had always known they were naughty, but now they had an entirely different meaning. And if boys got hard-ons talking dirty, that was okay. The words were *supposed* to make us bold and the girls shy. Actually, it made *everyone* bold — except the gays.

So what does a gay in junior high do in a small town? The same as non-gays: you masturbate. And in my case, it supplied the only consummation for a secret crush I had on a quiet seventeen-year-old Finnish boy on the football team. The next year I rather impulsively joined the junior varsity football team in hopes of seeing him naked in the locker room. While I was quite smitten by my youthful idol, it did not keep me from looking at the naked bodies of the rest of the team, or from having sexual fantasies about them. After practice I used to go home and masturbate in the bathroom before dinner. Eventually, I had my first sexual encounter with a boy I'd grown up with.

One day, as I sat on the school steps with him as he waited for his mother to pick him up, he turned to me and said, "Let's fuck."

"What?" I said, not quite believing my ears.

"You heard me," he said. "We could use a good *fuck*."

Not having done it with anyone yet, I couldn't have agreed

with him more — if he meant what I thought he meant. I proceeded cautiously, "You mean, the *two* of us?"

"Yeah!"

"You mean, the two of us *together*?" I asked nervously.

"Yeah!"

"But, I mean, we're both *guys*. . ." I began lamely.

"In the ass," he cut in impatiently. "We fuck each other in the ass!"

"Okay, when?" I said before he changed his mind.

"Tomorrow morning. Your place!" he shouted over his shoulder as he ran to meet his mother, who had just driven up.

The next day was Saturday, and my folks would be out of town. It would be perfect! But he never showed up. Several weeks later, we were up in his room playing Monopoly. We were alone in the house. He repeated the suggestion, and this time we did it. I did it to him first, then he did it to me. He was letting me do it to him a *second* time when we heard the front door slam! We jumped up, quickly pulled on our pants, and tried to act as if nothing out of the ordinary had happened.

By the tenth grade, it had become apparent that gays had two choices: you could become a "church fairy" — which meant no sex, you went to church a lot, and one of your dad's lodge brothers would give you a desk-job after you graduated. Or you could become a "bar fly." In that case, you could get sex — if you didn't mind the drunks that hung out in the bars.

Of course, if you went the *second* route, there was always the possibility that you'd be asked to leave town. Even if you weren't, the two alternatives seemed awfully limited — even with a dozen different denominations in town, and an equal number of taverns to choose from! I saw the handwriting on the wall: I'd best leave before I found myself forced into a choice I didn't want to make.

In the meantime, I continued to have sex with the same friend I had my first encounter with, and to the best of my knowledge, we were never detected. Neither of us developed any emotional or lasting sexual interest in each other. I certainly wanted to have sex and so did he — and we both knew the other would do it. Whenever his folks were out, he'd call and ask me over to watch TV. (My family didn't have TV yet.) All I had to do was slouch down on the sofa and spread my legs, and his hand would be over on my crotch. Then he'd unzip my pants, reach in, pull out my cock, and play with it while we watched the tube! Just when I'd think I couldn't hold back any longer, he would offer to let me fuck him, which I did. Sometimes we went up to his room, other times we got so hot we did it right there on the sofa.

This went on for about a year, then he started talking about girls. I wasn't about to go out looking for girls with him, so I suggested he fuck me. When he didn't seem very enthusiastic, I told him to close his eyes and pretend he was doing it to a girl. He did, but then he wanted to kiss, and I didn't. Not with him, anyway.

In the meantime, I was becoming more interested in doing it with other guys, but I was afraid of the rumors that would start about me. It was simply easier — and far less risky — for the two of us to keep on doing it with each other. His interest in having sex with me may have waned, but not his interest in having sex. Girls who would mess around could get any guy they wanted. And they had a definite preference for guys on the football or basketball team, which my friend definitely was not. While he never made the first move again, he never refused to go along when I did.

He may have thought about girls while we were doing it, but I knew I had absolutely *no* interest in trying it with one, and carefully avoided any situation where I might be forced into it. Fortunately, my parents never asked me why I didn't have a girlfriend, which took a lot of pressure off me. Still, it was a no-win situation. I didn't want to become the town whore but I wasn't interested in becoming its newest saint, either. My parents would have preferred me to be straight, but they would settle for saint — if that meant we wouldn't have to talk about it. We never did talk about it then — not ever, really. But as I said, I left as soon as I could. My folks wanted me to go to college, and I jumped at the chance.

Once, when I was home on break, I began asking my father about which friends were still around and what they were doing. I casually mentioned Jerry Kennedy. Jerry had graduated ahead of me, and I had heard things about him. My father looked uncomfortable, and wondered why I should ask.

"Oh, no special reason," I replied breezily.

Jerry had been on the football and basketball teams. I figured it was safe to mention him. Everyone knew him. Sullen, arrogant, he positively *oozed* sexuality.

"He's at Newberry," my father replied. Newberry was the state mental hospital. "Got to drinking, and pesterin' other guys. His folks had him committed."

I never mentioned his name again; there was no doubt what my dad had meant by "pesterin'." But Jerry had been so hot looking, the way he would strut around, his chunky little Irish ass bouncing insolently, and one of the few guys in the tenth grade who had enough facial hair to grow an honest-to-goodness mustache! And those black, flashing eyes....

That semester, I fell hopelessly in love with someone in my dormitory. Not only did I want to have sex with him, I wanted to make love to him. But nothing happened. Then during spring semester finals he asked if I would be his roommate next year, and I said yes. As it turned out, he reciprocated my feelings and we did make love together. Although he was reluctant to do more than indulge in a few furtive, guilt-ridden encounters, I was in heaven. I had found what I knew I had been instinctively looking for. It was not so simple for my roommate. He flunked out at the end of the year, and rather than face his family, ran off and joined the army. I was devastated.

My last year in college I knew I would have to tell my parents that I did *not* want to return home after graduation, but I dreaded it. Could I get away with not telling the *real* reason? If I went back, could I really live at home again? What about sex? Would they kick me out if I was sexually active? Even if they didn't, what about the town?

The questions remained unanswered. Actually, they never got asked. I got a job right after college with a company that moved me around to several midwestern cities. My first impression of gay life in these cities — in the early sixties — was *relief*! There *was* a place for people like me after all. I quickly learned I could do pretty much what I wanted. City neighbors had almost no interest, and even less control, over who you went to bed with.

That isn't all I learned. I remember walking down the street with a friend one Sunday afternoon in Indianapolis. We were on our way to a party when a young man leaned out the window of a passing car and let out a line of expletives ending in "fucking queers." Frankly, I didn't realize he was yelling at us. Not so my city-bred friend. He yelled right back, shaking his fist after the car.

Later, at the party, everyone thought it a very bold and foolhardy thing for him to do. I think a lot of gay people who grow up in small towns and rural areas are dumbfounded by the open hostility they find in the cities directed at gays. It wasn't like that back home for most of us. But was it because they accepted it? Or because we were still unsure of our sexuality when we left?

As I walked back to my office after lunch with my friend, I thought about my aunt's remark, and the woman who liked to kiss women. Rita was always cheerful and hearty. Especially compared with so many of the women in my hometown, saddled with children, with insensitive or abusive husbands, clothes to wash, and endless meals to cook. And there was something about this slim-hipped, big-bosomed woman that they responded to instinctively. Rita was not unfriendly to men, but her eyes would positively light up when one of these women said hello to her. She simply loved them for themselves.

As I sat down at my desk, I suddenly realized how much I envied Rita's rapport with these women. There was no man in my hometown even remotely her male counterpart. Undoubtedly some of that was because Rita was simply Rita, a wonderfully free soul, but she was also a woman. A man in the fifties wasn't allowed to feel about another man the way Rita felt about women.

Back then, the older men I met in gay bars seemed shockingly frivolous in comparison to someone like Rita. They were *not* warm and loving — they were absolutely obsessed with being found out and losing their jobs. They spent a lot of money sending drinks to young hunks they were afraid would otherwise have nothing to do with them, which was generally true enough. It was not so much that they were silly old men spending too much money, but they seemed to be so compromised by life. They made the men my age very uncomfortable — because if something didn't change, someday that would be our fate, too.

The Stonewall riots of 1969, thank God, changed all that. Still, it's not enough that construction workers wear their hair longer than most drag queens would have dared in the fifties! I wanted someone who would be more than a father, or a brother, or even a fuck-buddy. I grew up longing for the company of another male, someone who would have been allowed the same latitude women like Rita were given. Someone who could touch me, and teach me about myself. Today this seems even less likely than it did thirty-five years ago, considering what we now know about child abuse. Interaction between grown men and other, younger males is now more suspect than ever. Even if it were possible to isolate the sexual component from the rest of a young boy's needs and put it on hold, how can one possibly hope to allay the fears of a society where men are routinely abusive?

It's still a far from perfect world, but at least no one need spend life on the sidelines just because they are gay. Even if you're not especially good at asserting yourself, you don't have to settle for living an incomplete life. There *is* a gay world out there. And the rest of the world knows it!

Even though it's simply easier to be gay in a big city, there's something to be said for growing up gay in a small town, at least as I remember it in the fifties. Maybe I was just lucky. I had a father who believed in the equality of all people, and argued it with all the passion men in his generation brought to their convictions; and my Aunt Ann, who had the courage to tell a shy young boy the simple truth. Jerry Kennedy, who grew up only a few blocks from me, was not so lucky.

Growing up is a fearful business in any time or place. It's a wonder that *anyone* gets through it. But we survive. And when it comes time to make the important decisions in our lives — like coming to terms with our sexuality — all we need do is look to the example of the few, very special people who touched our lives. And then we can set aside childhood fears, take a deep breath, and get on with life.

▼

Wayland Harper*
Pittsburgh, Pennsylvania

My Foolish Heart

Tom Willard whizzed into and around my life for about six months after I returned to campus for my junior year in the fall of 1949. Always friendly, he recognized me from Harcourt's, a popular local drive-in where I worked the counter and set up trays. We had experienced an easy introduction. Early on I adopted his salty ex-Marine fatigues and cotton chinos without the back pockets as some of my own attire, but his black horn-rimmed glasses and frayed moss-green corduroy jacket with elbow patches gave him his own distinctive look. He had a pleasant mixture of the "Joe College" appearance, the "Artist" — his big expressive hands often carried dabs of color, and "The Stage" — he had picked up a certain flair in the drama department at school.

When I'd see him at the drive-in in the evening he was seldom with the same people. An active man on campus, he had many friends. Often he'd remain alone after his friends left, nursing a beer. He respected my need to do my job without interference, but was always ready to talk if I had a moment. Sometimes during our talks I'd get the feeling Tom knew me quite deeply, and his expression conveyed both amusement and acceptance. When I was busy and he could not bid his usual "See you, Way," in farewell, I was conscious that he always gave me a parting smile and waved his hand. After he was gone I would become aware of his absence, miss his scrutiny of my work, and inevitably experience a lag in my efficiency.

I was quite flattered and surprised when Tom asked if I'd like to go to Miami with him over a coming holiday.

"We'd hitchhike down on Friday after classes and have Saturday and Sunday at the beach," he suggested.

It had been years since I had hitchhiked any great distance. It would be fun striking out in a new direction and with someone as interesting as Tom. His name alone triggered something in me. I remembered another Tom who, as a kid, I had watched attentively on the basketball court and had felt a bit strange about. I had liked looking at him: his legs — that weren't skinny like mine — and his ass. I had once maneuvered to be alongside him and to look over at him at the urinal. I'd had a wet dream about him later, which stemmed from that view.

On Good Friday Tom and I made our way to Highway 92, each carrying a flight bag. We'd had little trouble getting away from campus. Soon after we arrived on Route A-1-A, outside of Daytona, the sun began to sink and it became quite cool standing at the roadside. A ride in an open truck brought us into Melbourne, a hundred miles short of our goal. Bouncing around in the bed of that truck, we had decided that we would check into a motel, warm ourselves with a Scotch, have some supper, and continue on our way early the next morning.

I had thought about our first overnight together. There was something about Tom that I could not fathom. He was full of surprises and kept my mind spinning to keep up. Throughout the afternoon our conversations had touched on the handsomeness of mutual friends, sex deviances reported about some Hollywood figures, and one's right to make choices. I couldn't remember ever feeling this free in talking with anyone before. Tom seemed to open me up in a way that I felt good about and had not experienced before.

The twin beds filled the small room we took for the night. Tom ran around in his shorts preparing for his shower. I had showered first, and was now in my pajamas and already in one of the beds, the one closest to the shower. When Tom finished in the bathroom he turned off the light, putting the room in total blackness. He walked around my bed, patting me on the belly, and got into the other bed. It was then that I realized what I had set up. Tom was the decision maker, the doer. I wanted him to make the decision to climb in my bed ... and start something. He had started something all right. His hand on my stomach had brought a quick erection. I turned to his side of the room, relieving some of the pressure against the covers, and I began to shiver as my inner warmth tried to dissipate itself. My teeth began to chatter and I felt I had to offer some explanation.

"I'm cold," I said. "It's cold in here. That drink didn't warm me up."

There was silence. Then Tom's deep, soft, stained-glass voice came from the darkness, "Do you want to come over here?"

Waiting for a couple of beats, knowing well my reply but not the magnitude of the step I would be making, an electrical charge suddenly bolted me out of my place. I could not have resisted.

"Yes, I do."

I opened his covers and placed myself on top of him between outstretched arms. Never having been invited into a bed, I felt drawn to Tom in a way I had only dreamed and I fell onto the path of my fantasy. My bare chest against his hot, hairy, completely naked body brought my mouth open in delight. He pulled my head down to his and found my lips with his mouth. I had never before felt the burr of a man's kiss, felt his mouth open under mine and his tongue thrust through to my teeth. It was all so positive and strong, his mouth pressed against mine indicating desire in a way I had never felt expressed. I opened my eyes, closed them in rapture, and opened them again, thinking: *Oh God ... Oh Tom! I've so wanted to do this. You're so great, so big, so hot, I love you.*

Part of me relaxed in the warmth and security I began to feel with his strength and tenderness. Another part tingled and wound tighter as I struggled to get free of pajamas while continuing the kiss and not losing body contact. Everything that I felt against me was exciting, the stickiness, the breathing, the confusion in our crotches.

When our lips parted I verbalized my last thoughts, "I love you."

Our bodies rolled each to a side and his hand reached for me and stroked my girth.

"Careful, oh careful, I'm so ready."

"Save it, save it," he said.

Discovering him, I gasped, "I have never..."

"You're just right," he said, repositioning himself around as I buried my face in the dense mass of moist hair surrounding his navel, relishing his majestic proportions and the smell of musk mingled with that of fresh soap.

Still hypnotized later, with Tom's eyes only inches from mine, the darkness around us seemed to be a blanket of light. My vision penetrated it and, as in a negative, his image stood out as if outlined in a heavy black line. The creases in his forehead gave his face character. I touched them and ran my fingers through his black curly hair.

"I can't tell you what I'm seeing and feeling," I said. "You, you are . . . just the best thing that has ever happened to me."

Tom smiled. Gold glinted from some back teeth and matched the one gold fleck in his blue eyes.

"I have never done anything like this before," I confessed.

"I know," Tom said. "Are you sorry? Didn't you want this to happen?"

"Yes, oh yes. I wanted something. I was so curious about you. I wanted to see you . . . naked. And no, I have no regrets. It is all so beautiful. You feel so good . . . and smell so good."

"Haven't you ever considered that these desires are natural for you, for me, for lots of others like us?" Tom questioned.

"No, I guess not. Are there lots of others? I was kinda hoping it was just you and me," I joked. "Who else do you know who is this way?"

"You've time enough to find out. There is a code in this new world you've entered. One doesn't expose one's friends . . . 'sisters'," Tom corrected.

"I'm not interested in them anyway. I know there is no one like you, no one who has anything like this!" I said, grasping.

This was a privileged position. I would have liked to hold on to this . . . this night forever. I would not let Tom sleep. Minutes after orgasm I could become excited again by Tom's barest response; a squeeze of the hand, a nestling movement of his body, or a leg thrown over mine.

From somewhere came the sound of music: a familiar tune that played from jukeboxes and had been repeated all day on car radios. The lyrics spoke loudly to me though they were issued faintly and from some distance:

> There's a line between love and fascination
> that's hard to see on an evening such as this,
> for they both give the very same sensation
> when you're lost in the magic of a kiss. . .
> But this time it isn't fascination
> or a dream that will fade and fall apart.
> It's love — this time, it's love
> My Foolish Heart

This was ours. There would be other love songs, other lovers, other days that I could not know. I knew only that I would associate and remember always Tom's faint smell of musk, this night, this moment, as "My Foolish Heart" beat next to him, hushed in his arms.

Don Sakers

Glen Burnie, Maryland

Stone Walls

It was five years after Stonewall, and I was a junior in high school.

Half a decade before, over four hundred gays had taken to the streets to protest the closing of the Stonewall Inn. How aptly gay-rights activists named that brief protest in the Greenwich Village summer of 1969: The Stonewall Riot. For it was like the smashing of a great stone wall across society, a bulwark of fear and prejudice, built to keep gays out. With Stonewall, the barriers were torn down and a new world arose.

As I came into adolescence, homosexuality was no longer "the love that dared not speak its name." Nor was it, as one commentator quipped, "The neurosis that would not shut up." The gay rights movement had done this: homosexuality could no longer be ignored; it could not be hushed up. The word "gay" was a permanent part of America's social consciousness. Whatever the others would do to us, they could never again pretend that we didn't exist.

Five years after Stonewall. The reds and oranges of autumn spread across central Maryland, and in my suburban Baltimore high school, classes were just beginning. Stonewall had torn down the major barriers in society, but I would still have my own stone walls to smash . . . or batter my head against.

The first was easy: recognizing that I could be attracted to other guys. The world of 1974 had prepared me for the concept; the books I read (mostly science fiction) led me to believe that most human beings were fundamentally ambisexual. By junior year, I was ready to admit to myself that there were boys I found attractive . . . and to take another little step toward the truth, by writing in my journal that "so far" there were no girls that attracted me.

I was on a collision course with the second stone wall. So far, I had just a teenager's unfocused sexuality; I still had not admitted to myself that I was exclusively gay.

The impetus to carry me over that barrier showed up quickly. My life changed that autumn. I had always been the outcast — I was bright, I read science fiction, I was no good at softball or basketball. I was prepared to remain an outcast forever . . . until I met a handful of others who were also outcasts. A dozen of us banded together and turned mutual loneliness into a unity that lasted far beyond our high school years.

It was a time of change, a time of possibilities, as we all learned to lower our defenses and open ourselves to one another. And in the course of this learning, something marvelous and terrible happened: I fell in love.

Fred was perhaps an unlikely choice for a first love — gangly, manic, highly intelligent yet very insecure. As I look at yearbook pictures and remember those days, I find it hard to believe that any of us were attractive, with our long, unkempt hair and our hysterical juvenile behavior. Yet we were all in the same condition; if now I can see through Fred's arrogant posturing, I can also understand the vulnerability and loneliness in which I saw a kindred soul.

Admitting that I was in love with Fred was easy. The rest wasn't — because I'd made the oldest mistake in the book. I'd lost my heart to a straight boy.

The first person I told was my best friend Ann. Her response was everything I could have wished for: supportive, accepting, and compassionate. During the next few months, as I worked through the difficult process of dealing with my first romantic interest, Ann was my sole confidant.

With the melodramatic instincts of teenagers, we at once decided that Fred must never know of my attraction to him. He might begin to wonder, we decided, if he had done something to encourage me . . . and while *I* was strong enough to face the fact of being gay, we had no such illusions about Fred's strength.

For months I struggled with my developing feelings. Once or twice, late-night parties turned into romantic sessions as boys and girls paired off to different corners of the basement for adolescent kissing and petting; I would sit quietly on the couch, watching Fred and his current girlfriend, and hold back tears of self-pity. Where *she* was, I wanted to be.

Eventually I was able to face reality and give up chasing Fred. By then, I was attracted to other boys and had enough to keep me busy without pining.

The happy ending to this story is that a year or so later I *did* tell Fred. He was flattered, although uninterested. Now, a decade later, Fred and I are still close friends.

As I dealt with my feelings for Fred, both Ann and I met the next, and most serious, stone wall: the one known as Ignorance. Neither of us had ever met a gay person, and our society provided us with few role models to show how gays were supposed to behave. I knew I wasn't a "sissy" and I knew that I didn't harbor a secret desire to be a woman. Beyond that, I knew nothing. Like so many gays before and since, I crept along in the darkness, alone. I was certain no one had ever experienced the feelings I was experiencing. Certainly no one had ever *said* anything about it.

Two things came together to build a bridge over that barricade of ignorance and loneliness: books, and current events.

It was the books that first provided me with good gay role models. Patricia Nell Warren's *The Front Runner* electrified me, ended my solitude, and gave me words for those feelings that I thought no one had ever shared. Mary Renault's *Fire From Heaven* and *The Persian Boy* told me what love between men could be at its best. Assorted short stories gave me glimpses of the strange, frightening and yet intriguing gay world. And Laura Z. Hobson's *Consenting Adult* was true ambrosia, nourishment for the spirit.

Then, as I started my senior year, Leonard Matlovich sued the U.S. Air Force. Matlovich, a decorated war hero, had been discharged because he wrote a letter to his commanding officer stating that he was gay. And then, amazingly, he dared to fight the Air Force across the front pages of the nation. In one fell swoop Ann and I discovered gay activism and encountered the thrilling concept that one could be strong, gay, and proud.

In the meantime, another stone wall stood before me, one that I would not succeed in passing for another decade. My father, snooping as many parents do, came across my private journal and read enough to realize The Awful Truth. After several angry and emotional confrontations, we made an unspoken agreement to ignore the matter. And ignore it we did. For the next few years, family dinners were perfectly cordial and civilized, but the entire concept of homosexuality sat unregarded in the middle of the table, right between the mashed potatoes and the peas. Only much later, after many storms and tears and much growing up on both sides, did my parents and I ultimately make peace.

But that was for the future. By the end of that wonderful and terrible year of 1975, I had emerged from darkness and ignorance into the bright light of full self-knowledge and pride. And Ann had accompanied me every step of the way. In my journal I could truthfully refer to myself as "young and beautiful and gay and proud."

The next barrier in my development was, in many ways, the most difficult one. Although I had been in love, I had not yet made love. I started college as a virgin, and remained that way through my entire freshman year.

It wasn't, in fact, until the summer of 1977 that I was to find my first lover, and give up that unwanted virginity.

I met Bill at a birthday party for a mutual friend. Fred and the others were well adjusted to my gayness, and they (and I) made no great secret of my sexual orientation. Bill kept quiet at the party, but called me the next day and we made a date. We spent a lazy summer afternoon rowing in the harbor, exploring downtown Baltimore and talking.

It wasn't until later, as I heard stories of other guys' first sexual encounters, that I came to appreciate how lucky I was with Bill. He was compassionate, gentle and very concerned with my feelings. He had suffered so much guilt at *his* first time, and he wanted to spare me that ordeal. As a result, it took me four days to convince him that I truly wanted him to go to bed with me.

That first experience, and the ones that followed, could not have been better. My parents were away at a baseball game; with Prokofiev and Wagner on the stereo, we made slow, gentle love together. Afterward we cuddled, showered, and left the house just as the last pitch of the baseball game was called on the radio.

Because of Bill's caring and his willingness to help ("If you'd rather be alone now, you can take me home; I'll understand," he offered), I suffered none of the guilt and anguish that many of my friends felt their first time.

Our relationship as lovers lasted three months. Despite some mutual friends and some of the same interests, we didn't have that much in common. We both knew that it was time to end it and move on to something else. Bill, compassionate as ever, let me down as gently as possible. For a year or so after, we stayed in contact and saw one another fairly often; then he moved away and my first love affair was completely done. Sometimes I feel left out, when discussion turns to the *angst* and pain of first love — but on the whole, I am happier that I had the good fortune to find someone like Bill.

There were still walls ahead . . . contacts with the gay world, the challenge of a mature, ongoing relationship between two adults, coming out dramatically and publicly as the author of a gay teenage romance novel . . . but the real struggle was over, for I had accepted myself. I now had an identity as a gay person.

A succession of stone walls . . . but these walls were not merely barriers to progress. Rather, they were like the stone walls at various levels of a terraced garden — and each wall passed took me further, lifted me higher, and revealed to me the splendors of yet another section of the garden. Looking back, some of the walls that took great effort to cross seem easy, and some scarcely seem like walls at all. Ahead there will be more walls, more effort, and gardens far more splendid than any that have come before.

Gene Davis*

Williamsport, Pennsylvania

Green Light

The stop light turned green. Mechanically, my right hand slipped the gearshift into first as my left foot eased out the clutch pedal. The car began to move, joining the rest of the traffic around me. Fortunately for the rest of the drivers on the road, I instinctively obeyed all the traffic laws and kept making all the right moves as I drove into the city. My conscious mind could not have been further from the operation of the car. Would Steve be home? Would I have the guts to go through with it? What would I say? What would *he* say?

I first met Steve in January of 1985. He had come to work at the consulting firm where I had been employed for about a year. He had just graduated from Penn State with a degree in psychology, but his heart had always been in the world of big business. He had heard about our firm, and about our internship program, and had asked my boss Phil if he could get into the program even though he had no formal education in business.

For those of us who worked at the firm, the term "intern" was synonymous with "gofer." Somebody had to do all those little jobs that the rest of us were too busy to consider. Most of the interns were just out of high school and looking for a chance to test the waters of the business game before deciding on what type of education to pursue. By virtue of his previous experience and his gift for communicating with people, Steve got the job.

Phil met me at the door as I walked into the office that morning. "I've got someone I'd like you to meet, Gene. I've just hired a new intern, and he'll be working with you for a while."

Just what I need, I thought. *Some new kid to show the ropes. Why do I always get stuck with this?* As Phil and I walked to the conference room, I was quite sure this was going to be another of those grin-and-bear-it things that you end up doing as a part of your job.

We entered the room, and I came face to face with one of the most attractive men I had ever seen in my life. Just over six feet, he had lots of beautiful blond hair, dark eyes, and a knockout face. Underneath jeans and a polo shirt was an athletic body obviously kept in good shape from lots of sports in high school and college.

"Gene, this is Steve. He's just starting in our internship program. Steve, I'd like you to meet Gene. You'll be working with him over the next couple of months."

"Hi, Gene," he said as he reached out to shake my hand. There was a warmth in his smile and a charisma about him that made my knees go weak.

"It's nice to meet you, Steve," I replied, being careful to look nowhere but at his face. Inside, my mind was saying, "Wow, is it going to be nice having him around the office!"

Meeting someone like that was always a mixed blessing for me. It was a genuine pleasure to meet a good-looking guy, and for a brief moment, it felt good to be attracted to him, but the good feelings always turned bad. Some little voice in the back of my mind immediately jumped up to say: *Now wait a minute, Gene. You're barely able to admit to yourself in some sort of abstract way that you're gay. You know you'll never be able to tell anyone. That would just shatter this wonderful bubble that you're living in. You've always been a good boy. You came from a good family that's well respected in the business community. You were second in your class in high school, and you graduated from Bucknell just like three generations of men in your family. You've always got more money than you really need. At twenty-nine, you've got more cars in your car collection than most people ever own in a lifetime. You're active in civic organizations. You're a Christian, Gene, and everyone knows that it's just not possible for a Christian to be gay. Everyone likes you. Why, they think you're just about the most perfect person they've ever met. One little slip, Gene, just one false move, and all this will come crashing down faster than the Hindenberg. You don't really want that to happen, do you? And even if you could somehow endure the loss of all that, everyone knows, Gene, that the only other homosexuals in the world are sickly young boys selling themselves on the street or dirty old men hiding in dark alleys waiting for a nice piece to come along.*

It was a very active little voice, and I hated hearing it say those things to me over and over again. Didn't it know that I knew all that stuff? Didn't it realize how much it hurt me? Couldn't it see that I had heard the message so many times that I was becoming more like it than me? Couldn't it understand that one more time, just one more time, and I might become so much like it that I would even consider destroying me?

Steve and I spent a lot of time together on the job. Our work involved quite a bit of travel, so we got plenty of time to get to know each other as we drove from place to place. I really enjoyed being with him, and he actually seemed to enjoy being with me. He was different from the other jocks I'd known in high school and college. This guy actually had a brain and could carry on a great conversation, and he didn't automatically write me off as a nerd the way the other guys did in school.

I still don't understand that. For some reason, in about sixth grade, I became the guy everyone loved to hate. If there was a practical joke to be played, I was always the victim. I was a star pupil in the classroom, but in the lunch room or the locker room, I was a non-person. No one would be caught talking to me.

Some other things also happened in sixth grade. The previous summer, I had met Mike and Bill when I joined a Boy Scout troop near my home. The three of us had a lot in common. We were all from socially prominent business families in the community, and we knew that we'd be in the same classes together in junior high since we were all college prep material. We did quite a few things together that summer like going to the movies, building go-carts, playing games, and all the other things guys that age do, never quite sure if we were boys or young men. The real problems started when we began to sleep out together in each other's back yards. It seemed so independent for us to be able to pitch a tent, stock up on candy bars and crackers, unroll our sleeping bags, and pretend we were miles from any other human beings, all the time knowing that Mom and Dad were less than fifty feet away just in case we really needed them. Maybe that feeling of independence was what got us in trouble.

It was only natural for guys our age to spend most of our time together talking about sexual things. Bill was the most physically mature of the three of us, with Mike next and me, as usual, last. After a couple of nights of just talk, we decided that maybe a little action wouldn't be so bad. It seemed perfectly normal to be curious about our own bodies, and about each other's, too. How did they work? What made them good? We decided to find out.

Although the idea seemed rather repulsive at first, it felt strangely good to touch Bill's body, and it felt equally good when he touched mine. I was fascinated by these new sensations. I had always enjoyed talking with Bill and Mike, and I really liked the social interaction when we did some activity together, but here was a wonderful new way of relating to my friends that I had never imagined before. It seemed like the perfect way to express our friendship on a new and exciting level. Needless to say, we spent several nights together over the summer, either in pairs or as a threesome, but I began to notice that my friends didn't fully share my attitudes about our activities.

Shortly after that, we all entered junior high school together, which was a frightening experience for me. Our school district had many elementary schools, but only one junior/senior high, so here I was suddenly surrounded by hundreds of faces I didn't know in an environment that I had never experienced before. Particularly threatening to me was gym class. We never had phys. ed. in grade school, unless you count recess. Now, here I was with thirty other boys confronted by Mr. Brewster, the gym instructor, who I was sure must have been right out of Marine boot camp. He scared the hell out of me. The first thing he told us was that next week when we came to class we should have the standard gym uniform, complete with a jock strap to protect the "family jewels." I had no idea what my grandmother's diamonds had to do with gym class, much less any notion of what a jock strap was. Fortunately, my mother did, and I showed up next week with all the required items, including the funniest and most embarrassing piece of underwear I had ever seen.

Sergeant Brewster said we were going to play basketball, which also scared me since I had no idea how it was done, and that we should line up against the wall and count off by twos. After that ordeal, I was ecstatic to find that both Bill and I were "ones." We separated to opposite corners of the boys' end of the gym, waiting for further instructions from Mr. Brewster. I was petrified. I stood next to Bill and asked what he knew about basketball. He didn't pay any attention. Why did we have to take gym class anyway? Who cares about the President's Council on Physical Fitness? I was getting worse and worse. My heart was pounding, my mind racing. This was too alien for me. I reached out and took Bill's hand.

At first, he pulled away, so I let it pass for a few moments. Then I reached out again, and this time he responded. It felt so very good to have that friendly touch. Maybe Bill was feeling as scared as I was, and welcomed the same feelings. But then it happened. The Sergeant saw us.

"Well, what have we here?" What could he be talking about? "A couple of pansies?" I had never heard the word before, so I had no idea what he was saying. "Holding hands is for sissies and girls." Now I knew what he meant, and immediately let go of Bill's hand, but it was too late. By now, the whole class — girls and boys — was staring at us. "Maybe you boys are in the wrong class." With that, he paraded us from the boys' end of the gym to the girls' end and made us stand there for the rest of the class.

I will never forget the looks on my classmates' faces as they returned to their activities, occasionally glancing over at us and snickering. Nor will I ever forget the look on Bill's face.

So the lesson was painfully learned. It was okay to express affection for parents. It was okay to express affection for other relatives. It was okay under certain strange guidelines, to express affection for someone of the opposite sex. But under absolutely no conditions was it ever even remotely okay to express affection for someone of the same sex. I think that's when I first started to hear that ugly little voice.

Steve and I were becoming really good friends. On the way home from a consultation one day, we decided that the firm owed us lunch, so we stopped at, of all places, McDonald's. As we were eating, the conversation turned to college life. Steve told me all the fun he had living at college, and I told him how much I thought I had missed by living at home and commuting.

"I think my junior year was the craziest," he said. "Six of us rented a three-bedroom apartment just off campus. There was me, four other guys, and another guy who was a homosexual." I just about choked on my Big Mac. "Guess which guy I shared a room with?"

A french fry stuck crosswise in my throat, but without batting an eye, I said, "the homosexual?" My lips had never uttered the word before. Would Steve be able to tell from the way I said it that I was one?

"You got it!" he replied. Something in the way he said it made me feel as though he was just making a statement of fact, and not an attack.

"Wow, what was that like? Did you have any problems?" I asked, meaning: did he try to jump you?

"It really wasn't a problem. The guy was a little strange, but generally okay. He used to bring some different and interesting people back to the apartment. Sometimes he'd be in drag, but not very often. Actually, he wasn't around that much. He was into drugs and having trouble with his classes, and eventually I think he dropped out."

I could hardly believe my ears! Here was the first person I had ever met who talked about someone who was gay and didn't immediately jump to words like "faggot" or "pervert" or "queer." I even detected a tinge of compassion in his voice as he talked about his roommate. Could it be possible that not everyone hated homosexuals? Could it even be possible that here was a person I could trust with my deepest and darkest secret? The little voice went into a frenzy at that thought.

I had a lot of trouble with the little voice over the next several weeks. It would not go away. All the other times, it would bug me for a few hours, or sometimes a day or two, but then it would go away. Not this time. It was all I could hear. It was all I could think about.

Sleep became impossible. Eating became a chore. Work became a prison. I started to notice a strange dull pain in my abdomen. Sometimes, it would go away if I ate a little something, but I wasn't eating for days at a time, so it was almost always there. I began to pop Rolaids like candy. I could go through a roll a day easily. Why couldn't that damnable little voice let me alone? I was entering a serious and dangerous depression.

People at work began to notice a change in me. At the time, I was 5'11" and about 156 pounds, but losing twenty pounds in a few weeks, it was hard not to notice a change. I would get to the office, sit down at my desk, and stare at the wall. Once or twice I would pick up a pen and try to write down a few things, but my hands shook so badly I couldn't read what I had written. Phil asked if there was anything he could do, but I defensively replied no. Steve was especially concerned and offered to talk with me at any time if I thought it would help. Parents and friends with good intentions tried to pry it out of me, but the little voice just wouldn't let me go.

I kept thinking about Steve. There was genuine understanding and love in his voice when he offered to talk. I began to remember one of our previous talks. We had been working on a big project together at the office, but we just couldn't seem to get anything done because of all the distractions of the day-to-day operation of the firm. We finally decided that we needed to work somewhere else. Since my parents owned a vacation home along the river just outside of town, and they weren't using it at the time, we retreated to that sanctuary to get some real work done. Steve said he would pick up a pizza and we could meet there around seven.

I got there first, and Steve arrived on time, pizza in hand. As we began to eat, it occurred to me that here I was alone with another man. Not just any man, but one I found incredibly attractive. We were actually sitting together on the same couch! It was a new feeling to me, but certainly not unpleasant or unwelcomed. But the little voice started up again, so I tried to concentrate on work. We got a lot done, then decided to just sit and talk and enjoy the solitude.

We began to talk about our pasts, and I discovered that Steve was not unlike me. He too had suffered rejection in junior high, but at least he knew why. He had grown up in a suburb of Philadelphia, and as he and his friends entered their teens, stealing became a way of gaining social acceptance. Not big things, not a lot of things, just a few little things. When Steve refused to compromise his values for the sake of his peers, they dropped him from their circle. Fortunately for him, he was able to make new friends and develop some strong, satisfying relationships with them. I shared with him my experiences in junior high, though not mentioning anything about Bill or Mike. He understood.

I had never felt so bonded to anyone before. We were so different in appearance and lifestyle and background, yet we had the same feelings inside. *So this is what it's like to have a friend,* I thought, *a real friend.* I had never had one before, and it felt so good to find one. It never occurred to me at the time, but I know now that it was more than friendship. It was genuine love.

But the voice kept at it. I decided to take a day off and go out to my workshop. When I got there, I started to tinker with one of the cars, but that didn't take my mind off the problems at hand. Then I tried some woodworking — sawdust therapy as they call it — but that didn't help either. The voice was louder than ever. *There's absolutely no way out of this mess,* it kept saying. It was a lose-lose proposition: I could spend the rest of my life listening to that horrid little voice, or I could let the secret out and ruin everything. Those were the only two choices.

Or was there a third?

I had always wondered what it felt like to die, and I had always wondered how anyone could be driven to take his own life. Now I knew: utter despair, complete hopelessness, total rejection, no options. If this was life, then I wanted no part of it. I had failed my parents by being gay. I had failed God by being gay. Worst of all, I had failed myself by being gay. It was time to cut my losses, as they say in the business world. There was no profit to be made from this investment, I decided, so perhaps I should get out of it. Surely my friends and family would be better off without me, since all I had ever done was to mess things up.

I dearly loved my cars, especially the convertibles. What better way to go than in one of the few pleasures I had enjoyed in life? Why, right there sat my favorite with the top down. With a heaviness that was indescribable, I made my way over to the car, opened the door, and sat down. The leather was so perfect, the chrome so bright. The paint reflected every detail of the room around me. I stared at the key in the ignition. It begged to be turned.

But my hand would not move. It just sat there, no matter what I commanded it to do. I fell against the steering wheel and wept uncontrollably. The little voice had a field day. *Not only do you not have the guts to listen to me,* it said, *or the guts to admit that you're gay, you don't even have the guts to go through with suicide.*

When I got to work the next day, Phil had laid a copy of a magazine article on my desk with a note that said, "This article really helped me. Maybe it will help you."

Most of us at the office share a strong Christian faith, and the article was from a magazine that we often had around. It was written by a well-known Christian author, and basically dealt with how to handle bad feelings and depression. Only one line from that article sticks in my mind, for it changed my life. "The first step in dealing with depression is total honesty before God, before men, and before yourself." I took the article home, and after reading it several times, I spent a lot of time being honest with myself about my sexuality. Then I spent considerable time being honest with God – for the first time in my life – about how it felt to be gay. Wonder of wonders, no lightning bolt struck me dead, but could I face the acid test of being honest before men?

The following day at work, Steve decided to take the afternoon off since he had worked most of the previous night. Before he left, he made a point of stopping in my office to say, "Look, Gene, I can see you're really hurtin'. I don't know what the problem is, or even if I can help, but I'm more than willing to talk with you any time about it. You know where I live, so please, for your sake, don't hesitate to stop by if you need to talk."

I decided right then that the time had come.

The next stop light turned green. Damn those stop lights. Why couldn't they just stay red? I'd rather sit right here for the rest of my life than go through with this. Instinct took over again, and before long I found myself turning into the alley behind Steve's apartment. Maybe his car wouldn't be there. *Wrong again, he's home.* I climbed the steps to his door without really knowing where I was, all the time rehearsing in my mind the carefully planned words I would say. Knock on the door. No answer. Maybe, hopefully, he went out, or could he be asleep? I turned to leave, somewhat relieved that there was no answer, but some force kept me from going down the stairs. Knock again, harder. It opened.

"Hi Gene! I'm glad you came over."

"Yeah. Hi." I could see from his eyes that he had been sleeping, but even the haze of just waking up could not hide the compassion in his face. We walked to the kitchen table of the one-room apartment where I had been a few times before. The place was familiar, but it took on a strange new meaning to me as I viewed it from a new perspective.

"You look really bad. Sit down. How about a glass of water?"

"Okay," I sat at the end of the table and went over again the well-chosen words I had prepared.

"Steve, there's something I've got to tell you. It's something I've never told anyone before in my life, so before I start, I have to ask you to keep all this in the strictest confidence. If anyone else ever knew about this, it would just destroy me. You've got the rest of my life in your hands."

"It's okay, Gene, you can trust me." I knew I could, but I had to say it anyway. My lips were as dry as parchment as my trembling hand reached for the glass of water. I began to stare at the floor, and my gaze fell upon a small kerosene heater in the middle of the room. It became the sole focus of my attention, and I can still recall every detail of it. Still staring at it, I began, "Steve, I'm not the person everyone thinks I am. I'm. . ." Where were all those words I had planned? I couldn't seem to remember a single one.

"Gene, are you sure you really want to tell me?" I wondered if he was concerned for me, or if he really didn't want to know the truth.

"I have to say this. If I don't, I'm gonna go insane."

"Okay. Just take your time. There's no rush." The tone of his voice was a great comfort.

"There's something about myself that I've always kept hidden, and telling someone about it after all these years is the hardest thing I've ever done. Steve, I'm . . . I'm gay." I could hardly believe that I was hearing that word in my own voice. Silence followed. "I've never really had sex with another man, other than a few adolescent experiments in junior high." Bill and Mike. "But I'd like to," I added, wanting to be sure that I made myself clear, my eyes still firmly planted on that heater lest I see the reaction in Steve's face. "You can't imagine what it's like to go through your entire life, and never let anyone know that. I feel so bad and dirty sometimes that I can hardly stand myself. That's what's been bothering me these past few weeks. It's always been hard to deal with, but recently, it feels like there's a war going on inside me. Frankly, I don't even know why I'm telling you now. I've only known you for a couple of months, but for some reason, you seemed like the only person I could ever tell. I know you'll never be able to think about me the same again." Silence again.

"Well, Gene. . ." The words were slow and deliberate. My mind braced for the rejection that the little voice promised me would come. ". . .I want you to know that I'm really honored that you chose to tell me, and as for how I think about you, I respect you now more than I ever did before. It took a helluva lot of courage for you to say that."

Could I believe my ears? His words sounded accepting, but surely his face would give him away. My eyes had been so glued to that heater that it was difficult to get them to look elsewhere, but slowly I turned to look at Steve. His face never lied, and I could see the same friendship, the same understanding, the same love I had seen there before. I almost cried at the sight.

"Steve, did you ever suspect that I might be gay?"

"Well, to tell the truth, the thought did cross my mind. But homosexuality is no big deal to me, and it shouldn't be to you either. A person's sexual preference is a very private matter, and no one should interfere with you making your own decision. Being gay's not right for me, but if it's right for you, then that's all that matters."

"You know, I never chose to be gay. I've tried lots of times to change, but it just doesn't work."

"Let me ask you a question, Gene. If you had all the power in the world, and you could change anything about your life you wanted to, would you use that power to make yourself straight?"

"Well, I don't have that kind of power, but if I did, I honestly don't think I'd use it."

"Good, and don't let anyone else tell you otherwise. It's your life and your decision."

"Man, I can't tell you how much better I feel. It's like I'm suddenly alive again!"

"I'm glad to hear that, Gene, but you've gotta remember, this is just the first step. You've got a long road to travel until you can completely accept all this. In fact, tomorrow you'll probably be asking yourself why you ever told me, but you took the right step — a big step — probably the biggest you'll ever take, but it's only the beginning. Just remember that if you need to talk about it, and you will, I'm here."

It felt so good to finally be in the open about some of my feelings, even if it was with only one other person. Even my body began to feel better, and that little voice didn't seem to be such a problem, at least for the moment. I didn't want to leave, so I was really glad when Steve suggested we go out for dinner. We drove to our favorite Chinese restaurant.

It was a little strange sitting there in the restaurant. I couldn't help wondering what other things Steve might be thinking. I also wondered if the other people in the place could tell that I was gay. Did finally saying it make me somehow look gay? Was Steve embarrassed to be seen with me now that he knew? Would I ever have the courage to tell anyone else? All I knew at that moment was that I was glad I told Steve, and that from our dinner conversation, I was sure he really did care about me in the same way as before.

As we rose to leave, Steve said, "Hey, don't forget your fortune cookie!" I've never been one to put much stock in fortune cookies. I usually like their taste, but the messages always seemed so hokey and contrived. After all, these things were made miles away by people who never met me, and who couldn't have been sure I would get a particular cookie even if they did have a specific message for me.

But I do believe that, from time to time, God can choose some very different ways to get His message across. I cracked the cookie open, and had most of it eaten by the time I unfolded the message.

As I read it, not expecting to get much out of it, I was suddenly struck by the meaning of the words I saw printed on that tiny piece of paper:

"Depart not from the path which Fate has you assigned."

Wayne A. Ferris

Mission, Kansas

Coming Out — Late

In February of 1976 I came out — at the age of fifty-seven. My coming out was a sudden thing. I had never thought about it or planned it, I'd never even heard the phrase. It was an irresistible urge; an unseen hand that pushed me out of the house. I have often wondered what caused it at that late point in my life. Maybe the couple of *Advocate* issues I'd seen had raised my consciousness. Or maybe my brain had just rebelled at the hermit I'd become.

My upbringing was not unusual. I was the youngest of five children, four boys and a girl, raised in a town of two hundred people in the center of South Dakota. My family was not religious, but I went to Sunday School and Epworth League and sang in the choir because there was nothing else to do.

I played with dolls surreptitiously with little girl friends until I was in the sixth grade. I knew it was discouraged for a boy to do that, but for me it was a compulsion. I started to realize by the age of twelve that I was different, and was already called "sissy" fairly frequently. I played basketball as a high school freshman and was complimented on my ability by the coach. But I dreaded the locker room — I wanted to examine the others, but feared the erection that was likely to follow. As a result, after a practice or game, I usually ran three blocks home to bathe.

The town had a library, but the donated books and those on loan from the state library were unlikely to contain anything about homosexuality. Asking for such a book would create news that would soon spread all over town. The only such reading I remember was from a pulp detective magazine which told me (1) I could not possibly evade the police, and (2) I would attack a child — probably a relative. That information was terrifying for a person who thought he was the only weirdo in the state.

My last years in high school were a nightmare of fear, and many nights I cried myself to sleep, wondering what was to become of me. I couldn't wait to graduate and leave town, for fear I might go suddenly insane and attack a small niece or nephew.

I attended a business college in Sioux Falls for several months in 1938, after which I was offered a job. While working there I met a grocery clerk, older than I was; he became very friendly with me and my mother, who lived with me during the winter. One day he suggested that we go to a dance that night, and my mother, who probably wondered why I never dated, encouraged me to accept. Ralph suggested that, since we would be getting home late, I should plan to spend the night at his place, just a few blocks down the alley from where I lived. I accepted, and when we got together that evening, Ralph suggested that we go to a movie instead. We did, and then went to his place for a glass of wine. He wanted me to stay all night, but the hour was early and I went home. I could kick myself for not taking that opportunity to start my gay education earlier.

Two years later my employer went out of business and I went with friends to Los Angeles looking for work.

While I lived in Los Angeles I had my first gay sex — at the old Request Theater near Pershing Square. An older man sitting next to me fondled me under my hat, and I did the same for him. He then got up and left, but came back shortly. I now realize he expected me to follow him to the john, and when he returned he'd have nothing to do with me. I hung around outside the theater for the following three nights hoping to get another glimpse of him.

In my early twenties, I read a newspaper article by a psychiatrist who discussed making gay men straight by the use of hypnosis. I found the name of a psychiatrist in the phone book and went to him. He knew nothing of the hypnosis therapy I'd read about, but took me on as a patient because I was still having hetero- as well as homosexual dreams. After several sessions he decided he could do nothing for me, and ended by trying to help me develop a more masculine walk and voice.

While in L.A. I was called up by the draft, and then rejected, but no one told me why. A few years later I accepted a secretarial job in Saudi Arabia for the Arabian American Oil Company. It was near the end of World War II and all the executives' wives and female workers had been returned to the U.S., so all the secretarial, nursing, and other typically feminine positions were filled by men, most of them gay. I was still closeted, but many recognized my orientation and talked openly around me about gay social life, who had crawled into bed with whom, and so on. I was invited to the weekly parties, but was never able to make myself attend.

After two years on the Persian Gulf coast, I was transferred across the country to the Red Sea, where I spent the last six months of my contract. There were few Americans there — we hobnobbed mostly with the British, and the employees of other English-speaking legations. There was no entertainment, other than the parties that were thrown almost every night. It was at one of these parties that *it* happened.

It was the old "across a crowded room" story. He was a secretary for the U.S. consul, my age, handsome, and certainly more experienced than I was. For five months we were together every spare moment, night and day. But after one of our parties, he was found by the servants — passed out and "exposed." I was mortified, and didn't see him very much after that. After I'd returned to the U.S. I realized how lopsided the relationship had been: I had been infatuated, he'd never laid a hand on me. I was simply his choice of what was available.

I returned to Kansas City, and attended the Art Institute, where I earned a degree in fashion design in 1951. While attending school I lived with two fellows with whom I was very close — so close that I had no desire for homosexual contact — but after they left for out-of-town jobs, I went for a short time to gay bars and cruised the Liberty Memorial. Still I was closeted, and homophobic. A complete stranger with effeminate mannerisms sent me scurrying to the other side of the street to avoid a face-to-face meeting. I lived alone and cruised a shopping center and was very promiscuous.

In 1970, after many years of this, I withdrew into myself and became a hermit. I went to work faithfully and put in a lot of overtime. Then I would go home and read or work on crafts. I became very frustrated and, since I had no gay friends to talk to, I picked a psychiatrist out of the phone book and went to him. I talked my head off, which helped, but what I needed was to meet other gay men and he couldn't — or wouldn't — help me.

I went to several different psychiatrists after him, and my fourth, a gay man himself, really helped me. He told me I was starting the coming out process — I'd never heard the term before. I'd gone to the Metropolitan Community Church, joined the Gay People's Union and gone to a couple of bars. I was extremely happy, but wondered what was happening to me.

In 1981 I retired from my job with thirty years of service. By that time I was perfectly comfortable with myself and my lifestyle. Coming out gave me a feeling of happiness I'd never dreamed of. I'd never really had friends before, and those first gay friends are still my closest.

Coming out also awakened a tremendous curiosity in me. I've attended gay conferences all over the United States, where I've heard fascinating speakers, and I started buying books and now have a large gay library.

I've never had a relationship, since the one in Saudi Arabia. I've looked back at the times when one might have been imminent, and have discovered that I've unconsciously run away. But probably the most consoling thing in coming out was the realization that I was not alone. We are many and we are everywhere — but I had never guessed that the number could be as high as one in ten.

My parents are now dead, as well as a brother and a sister, but I am out to my two remaining brothers and their families. I'm also out to many friends of high school days, and I feel sure the news is out all over the small town where I was raised, but nothing is ever said.

I still get a charge out of coming out — I did it recently to an old family friend. He seemed incredulous and changed the subject, not because I was gay, but because I was willing to put it into words. Even with strangers, I feel I'm letting them know there's one more gay man in the world than they might have previously thought. Each time I come out it further builds my self-esteem.

I feel sure that if I had not come out when I did, I would not be alive today. I don't think I could have taken much more of that solitary life. Now, since I work on the gay talk line and with people with AIDS — many of whom are still in the closet — I can help others come out before they waste as much of their lives as I did.

▼

Gary M. Spahl

Boston, Massachusetts

Ocean Park

It was yet another perfect weekend during the warm and sunny summer of 1985. We were in Ocean Park, a small hamlet on Martha's Vineyard – a sweeping cluster of Victorian-era, gingerbread-style homes, looking out on a grassy common and beyond to the Atlantic. With a gazebo and geese and the whitecaps flirting across the water, it was classically charming and beautiful.

The grass was browning and brittle, tired from salt, wind and August sun. We sat, drinking beer, enjoying the space and the day. She was living on the island, and I was ending what would probably be my last visit of the summer. In a few hours the ferry would take me home to the city. It was sad to be leaving – both the island and my friend.

We first met at work, in a restaurant. We were both finishing college, and seemed to be the only ones capable of tolerating each other's senior year bitching. We'd rant endlessly about deadlines, wisecrack our way through the standard restaurant mania, then go out for drinks afterward and rant and wisecrack some more. She served. I bussed. Together we made good money. I liked her.

Unlike most workplace friendships, this one continued after our employment ended. With work no longer a common topic, our conversation expanded. She was an artisan and I was a writer, and we had long, soul-searching discussions. About the creative curse of achieving success only by refusing to be satisfied with your work. About family and friends. About hopes and fears and ideals. About whatever else it is that good friends talk about.

She was intelligent, and kept my brain from falling asleep at the wheel. She was creative, and could empathize when sympathy wasn't enough. She'd had a lopsided share of tragedy in life, yet was always positive and upbeat and encouraging. I realized how important she was to me after she moved to the island.

I had come out to a few people, and was still quite new to the game. Positive reactions were reassuring and relieving; negative ones hurt. Good-byes are always sad — sudden, permanent good-byes are heart-wrenching. It was time to tell my island friend — to strengthen an already solid relationship, or to cut loose while there was still emotional time.

I had tried to tell her many times during this visit. On each attempt, something balked. How do I start? What if she hates me? It's not the right place. Right time. Right mood. Anxiety was high, for the risk was great. She was an important person in my life. A loss would be devastating. This was a big one, and could lead to a big hurt.

Sailboats lounged on the horizon. The sun whispered of lazy island heat. The beer was wet and warming — and went down easily. We talked. About our work, our family, our lives. It was not a trivial conversation — we would not be seeing each other for some time.

I tried to find a good place to start — a key transitional phrase or a brief lapse. My head spun with fears and hopes and scenarios. Outside, my body kept talking and listening and gesturing. Inside, my blood ran cold . . . hot . . . cold. My feet went numb, then my hands, then my feet again. She talked, I listened. I talked, she listened. Ocean Park disappeared. The Atlantic disappeared. Breathing became difficult. Every cell screamed with anxiety. My heart pounded furiously. Throat and lungs swelled with unspoken words, waiting for release and acceptance — bracing for hurt and anger. The beer wasn't cold. It wasn't warm. It wasn't wet or dry. I chugged like a madman, I talked, I listened. She talked, she listened. The sailboats hung precariously on the edge of everything.

It came from nowhere, from everywhere. We were talking about relationships — whose I can't remember. It just fell into the conversation, unannounced, unplanned, unexpected.

". . . Yeah, like, I've been seeing this guy for a couple of months now, and sometimes you just gotta take things as they are."

From the ocean, I watched myself say the words. From the gazebo, I heard myself say them. What was I doing? Not like that. Not without a preface, a warning. Not just thrown into the middle of a conversation. I blew it!

"Uh-huh," she said, "but she doesn't have to put up with some of the games he plays."

"Uh-huh," she had said. She didn't miss a beat, just kept on talking. "Uh-huh." Was that it?

"Did you hear what I just said?"

"What?"

"That I've been seeing another guy?"

"Yeah."

"That doesn't shock you? Doesn't bother you? Are you surprised?"

"I know you. I think I know what you like. People are people. You know that doesn't bother me."

The Atlantic Ocean reappeared. The beer turned wet. My body resumed normal operations.

We talked. About being gay, about being straight. A close woman friend from childhood recently told her she was involved with another woman. Though understanding, she was still upset. I told her to be strong, to be patient. To treat her friend no differently, yet not pretend the issue didn't exist. I consoled and supported her — a startling role reversal, I thought, given the situation. And by suggesting how to cope and deal with her gay woman friend, I was explaining how her gay male friend expected to be treated.

The sun and conversation shifted. We talked about the creative curse. Life on the island. Life in the city. The weather, the world, and whatever else it is that good friends talk about.

My ferry was leaving shortly. She had to get ready for work. She drove me to the dock. We exchanged a kiss and a hug, and my "Thanks" covered more than her hospitality.

The ferry rumbled on toward the mainland. Watching the island fade into the sea, I savored warm memories and banished thoughts of work until the next day. I turned to feel the wind and the spray on my face. The water sparkled brilliantly in the late afternoon sun. Yes, I thought, it has been a wonderful summer.

▼

Saavan*

Beverly Hills, California

A Leopard and a Madman

I flinched when his hand touched mine. He looked me in the eye, standing only inches away. My white pullover shirt lay on the bench behind me, his scuffed jersey was draped atop the half-wall of metal lockers. My eyes searched the length of the locker room, though I was certain we were alone. At that moment my entire P.E. class was puffing and panting on the football field. I had been excused early for an appointment. I was not aware that he had also requested an early leave and followed not far behind me. When he entered the room, I was standing behind a section of lockers, fully naked. Quickly I struggled into my jeans, banging my knee painfully on the metal bench. The hardness between my legs had been instantaneous and I feared he might catch a glimpse of it. When he walked past his own locker, sliding the blue jersey over his head, I shuddered involuntarily. Now he reached out for me and I stood mutely, unable to return his touch, unwilling to pull away.

His name was Jason. He was blond, blue-eyed, beautiful. He was white, like all the other faces floating in my daydreams. For months I had watched him, created fantasies around him. Never did I guess that he was aware of my attention, that he wanted me also. Now as his fingers caressed mine, the fear that immobilized me surrendered to desire. I caressed him in return, our lips came together and our hands explored furtively. For a time the world ceased to exist. But as strong as our desire was, we did little beyond kissing and caressing. Equally fearful of being discovered, we soon pulled apart. Hastily we clambered into our clothes. Whispering in an empty room, we made plans to meet that night. We kissed one final time as if to reassure ourselves of what had just happened. As I walked out of the building, I was certain that my most intimate fantasy was about to be realized.

That night we met in the deserted school parking lot. Jason owned an old black-topped Mustang. I climbed in and we fled into the shadows of the countryside. We sat in silence, neither one reaching out to touch. Once we got out of the car, it was as if the sky was bursting after a long drought. We were mad in our desire to touch, to hold. Being entangled in a sixty-nine position in the middle of a peach orchard was not how I had visualized my first encounter. But the hunger of his hands, the echo in my fingertips soon chased away any such thoughts. It was the first time I had touched another man sexually, the sensation surpassing anything I had ever conjured in my numerous fantasies.

After we pulled apart, lying stretched out on the old sheet he had the foresight to bring, I had a million words to share. There was no feeling of guilt or regret on my part; years of loneliness had given me ample time to work through such emotion. But I did not share my thoughts, for Jason quickly withdrew into himself. He offered no reason, I did not press the issue. I did not have to. Even in the feeble light of the waxing moon I could see the confusion in his eyes. He was at war with himself, locked in a battle I was just putting behind me. He responded to my touch half-heartedly now and I realized that reality would not be as simple as the fantasies in my mind had been. And this first night set a precedent. Each time we met, it was under cover of darkness, always searching out some remote sanctuary. I was disillusioned by his paranoia and yearned for a love he was unwilling to share. Yet I could not say no to these hours of furtive sex, for I was ruled by need. And confused as he was, his desire surmounted his fears enough to meet me often.

Ours was a quite one-dimensional bond. At school we did not

acknowledge each other. All was as it had been before, and it left me feeling rather empty. In many other ways I was blind to Jason's shortcomings. I knew but one facet of the boy but that one was sufficiently powerful to overshadow all else. For a while.

One day, as I was passing through the student square, I witnessed a scene that rudely opened my eyes. Jason and two other white youths were taunting a dark-skinned boy and I heard the lips that so often touched mine call the silent youth a "raghead."

I was filled with rage and revulsion. How could he? The word stung me, though it had been directed at another. Throughout the day it echoed in my ears — and yet I did not hesitate to meet Jason that night. Later, as my body rose above his, as my crotch crashed feverishly against his ass, the pain of the silent youth was the farthest thing from my mind. But it was the first image to invade my thoughts as I lay exhausted afterward, my head resting on Jason's arm. *Raghead.* How many times had I trembled at the utterance of that word?

One moment I saw the dark-skinned youth wince as Jason hurled his insult. The next moment it was I who was being taunted: nine years old, not knowing a word of English. Lifted out of a small agrarian village in northern India in 1968, I had been thrust into a culture that was as alien as the white faces that swarmed about me. Life might have been easier had my parents settled in an urban, more enlightened city. But they relocated to Yuba City, a mound beside the road in rural northern California. In this town my grandfather had lived for some forty years, farming a few acres of peach and prune trees. Yuba City was an overgrown village, its main streets lined with majestic gas stations and hamburger joints. For the first few months I pleaded with my parents to send me back to India, to allow me to live with my uncle. My new surroundings seemed hostile and I understood little. My classmates thought it wonderful sport to tease the shy, strange new kid. They would stand around me, uttering words I did not comprehend. Someone would snatch my lunch pail and an impromptu game of keep-away would commence. I did understand their derisive laughter. I tried to bite back the tears, losing the struggle in the end.

To blunt this new pain I began to withdraw into myself. I never told my parents of the situation at school; it was difficult to share what I saw as shame. I learned quickly that the more I became like these Americans, the less abuse I suffered at their hands. The shedding of my Indian identity became Rule One of survival. Within two years I was speaking my new language with confidence and surpassing most of my classmates academically. Slowly I began to make friends, taking care that all of them were fifteen shades lighter than me. I neglected my mother tongue, Punjabi, to such a degree that I soon lost the ability to read and write it. Whenever possible, I avoided being seen in public with my family. I would rant at my father for walking into the front yard clad in his *dhoti*, the skirt-like wrap worn by many north Indian men. And I was thrilled when someone mistook me for anything other than Indian. Yet my efforts at gaining acceptance lessened my persecution only slightly. There was still the name calling, the hostile stares and threats, the condescension that required no words. Most of the other Indian kids formed their own clique, turned to one another. I shunned them entirely. So I walked in a no man's land. Nightly I would fantasize about having blond hair and blue eyes. I learned well the lesson of self-hate.

Lying beside Jason, as those images washed over me, I looked into his eyes, wondering what insanity lay inside. How could he hate that youth for being Indian yet lie here beside me? And how could I respond to his touch, knowing of his bigotry? I opened my mouth to voice my doubts but did not break the silence. What if he turned away from me? I was addicted to his touch. I fancied that I loved him and I did not want the connection severed. I swallowed my pride, something long practiced, and I held him tighter. He returned the pressure wordlessly as was his habit. Little did he know that, more than wanting him, I wanted to *be* him.

Jason and I began our relationship in late October. By the end of January we had fallen into a routine of meeting three or four times a week. As the weather turned colder, we were forced to make do with the back seat of the car. It was cramped, limiting, but it was better than not touching at all. Our interaction did not grow into anything beyond the sexual, though we shared a bit of affection before and after. Not fully satisfied, I soon dropped any romantic aspirations I had held for Jason. My crotch was quite satisfied by his touch but my heart began to weave romantic fantasies around other faces. The blinders had fallen from my eyes. And it was during this time that I saw a face I must have surely overlooked before. It was in the middle of my senior year that I encountered my leopard.

His thick ebony eyebrows arched above dark brown orbs. He had an exquisite face, finely crafted, with high cheekbones and sharply-defined lips, and a thick head of hair that was in startling contrast to his dark features: honey blond, parted in the middle and feathered back as was the rage in 1976. His name was Don; he was then sixteen years old. He was slightly built, but that did not bother me. It made him seem more vulnerable.

Did he harbor the same feelings I did? I could not be certain. From the first time I noticed him I sensed a sadness in his eyes, but that was not enough to convince me. Now when I think about his gentleness, his grace of movement, I have no doubt he and I shared the same secret. But at that time fear gripped me each time I thought of approaching him. What if he did not like Indians? There was always that consideration. So I watched him. He became a central figure in my numerous fantasies. With him I shared all that I could not share with Jason.

Many times as I lay beside Jason, my thoughts would dance around the memory of Don's face. We were sitting in a cinema, our hands clasped, our shoulders brushing in the darkness. We sat sharing dinner at some restaurant, our knees touching under the table. On and on my thoughts would fly. Then the body beside me would move, the fantasy would dissolve. I would look at Jason critically then, wonder if he would ever get over his fears enough to allow us such moments together. What was it that hindered his acceptance of himself? Surely the realization of his attraction to men could not have been any more difficult than the shattering experience I remembered!

I was a boy still reeling from my daily bouts with racial hatred when a new shadow had fallen upon my world. Pleasure it promised — pain it guaranteed. I found my eyes following the slender bodies of my male classmates. *No*, I thought, *it cannot be. It is admiration I feel for them, nothing more.* I was puzzled one morning when I woke to find my underwear sticky, clinging. There was a vague memory of some pleasurable sensation during the night. Soon I discovered that I could create this sensation merely by touching my crotch, an almost unbearable ecstasy when I stroked my penis to climax. Images would form in my mind as I played with myself. Always male. Always white. I shuddered at the realization and sensed that I could not speak to anyone about this. Something was wrong with me. What would the world around me think if it found out? Never mind that this world had never really accepted me as one of its own; I did not wish to be cast out any further. So I snapped the locks into place and imprisoned my desires.

For a time I hoped it was a phase, this attraction to men. Perhaps it was something purely American and, as an Indian, I would be touched by it only fleetingly. Certainly I had never heard the subject mentioned by any Indian I knew. But the fascination not only lingered but grew in intensity. I decided that I must rid myself of it consciously. Stroking myself behind the locked door of a bathroom, I would fantasize madly about women. Sometimes I would take with me a purloined photo of some *Playboy* centerfold. As soon as I lost myself in the sensation, however, hairy chests and hard cocks would once again fill my mind. Athletes, actors, faces on the streets, boys I shared class with. They would wander in and out of my thoughts. And I would be disgusted. I had found one more reason to hate myself.

When I found that my feelings would not be purged, I became terrified. For the next two years I continued to battle them, and try to reshape them somehow. It was not until the age of fourteen that I came to accept the permanence of my strange attraction. Still fearing the stigma of being a faggot, a word used regularly on the playgrounds, I decided that I must be bisexual. It was a comfortable shield to cower behind on my internal battlefield; I could still claim to be pseudo-normal. I ignored the effort it took me to even consider a woman sexually. I visualized myself in the future, suppressing my desire for men. I would settle down with a woman of my parents' choice, as my brothers were doing, and I would raise a family. No one ever need know the truth. How ludicrous the image seems now. How comforting it was then. The world was bombarding me with terrifying images of homosexuality, and I shrank from them. No, that could not be me. There were no healthy homosexuals on television, or on the big screen. There were no songs about men loving men, or books about such romances. My feelings of isolation grew.

My Indian heritage exacerbated my turmoil. My parents, though kind and loving, had definite expectations of me. I was their youngest son, their bright hope. In their eyes floated visions of their seventh child mounted atop a white horse, a bride clad in the matrimonial crimson *sari* of India seated behind him. How could I shatter that dream? For all their gentleness, I knew that they would never accept homosexuality. The only Hindi word I had heard used in reference to people like me was when I had recently heard one man call another a *goonda*. Defiled. Unclean. That was their son. That was me. No, they must never know. I bolted the door more tightly, retreated further into my crevice.

Then came the first year of high school. What elation, what terror, to walk into a men's locker room for the first time. The only nudity I had witnessed was what I fashioned in my daydreams. I was momentarily lost in a sea of naked, ripe asses and bouncing cocks. Were it a fantasy, I would have reached out in all directions. But it was reality and I was petrified of my secret being discovered. It was torturous for me, listening to an acquaintance chatter about the chances of the Oakland Raiders making the Super Bowl while his cock dangled within reach of my itching hand. I wished I could reach for it, I wished I could grab with both hands the ass parted in front of me as my neighbor bent over to pick up a shoe. My body would go rigid with tension each time I walked into the gym. I was morbidly convinced that my penis, which seemed to have a mind of its own, would one day rise to full salute for some hard enticing body. So my eyes learned to caress the floor.

The first three years of high school passed uneventfully. I had numerous crushes, none ever leading to anything. There was an occasional date with a girl, over my mother's objections. She was afraid I might become entangled with an American girl. For me it was merely a means of social contact, the dates never leading to physical contact. My friends were beginning to express and pursue their interest in girls, adding to my isolation. For me there were the frequent bouts with tears in the sanctuary of my bedroom, hands beating pillows, hurling books across the room. I shredded and discarded pictures of Vishnu, Krishna and other hindu deities for prayers unanswered. And I prayed incessantly to the American God whose existence I doubted. I prayed that I might awake the following morning and find that my secret was just a bad dream.

Sometime in the middle of my junior year I dropped my charade of bisexuality. The lie had grown too heavy. Finally I admitted to myself that I felt no attraction to girls. I was a homosexual. I was a fag. This was one of the lowest points of my life. I felt worthless. I was forever afraid that someone would see through my facade of normalcy. I told queer jokes, and each time I did, I would hate myself a little bit more. Was there no way out? Would I be locked behind this wall for the rest of my life? And what of love? Was I ever to know that emotion?

It was near the end of this year that I came across the Kinsey study on sexuality — ten percent of all human beings were thought to be homosexual. I was not alone! In my class there must be sixty of us! But who were they? I would peer into the faces of my classmates, hoping to recognize something familiar. But of course I saw nothing; I had no idea what to look for. *Where are you?* I wanted to scream out from the student square. Though I did not meet another homosexual, I was now convinced that someday I would meet them, these invisible people. The isolation subsided and I began to work my way out of my dark crevice.

The seed planted in my junior year bore fruit in the next twelve months — 1976-77; the year of Anita Bryant's message of hate; the year John Briggs tried to bar homosexual teachers from California classrooms. It was a climate of hate yet I found nourishment amid the poison. I was outraged, filled with hostility. But now these emotions were not directed inside. It was the world around me that I wanted to tear apart, finally seeing that the darkness I floundered in was of its design. With homosexuality splattered across the front page I was force to face my own demons. And I did. Once I had shrunk from such headlines, now I would seek them out.

Most of my reading on homosexuality was done with an air of secrecy. I was willing to admit the truth to myself, but I could not yet share it with the world. So I would check out the magazines and books, and find an isolated corner in which to devour them. I would cover the title with my hand, my eyes would flit about the room, making certain I was not being watched. I learned about the battles waged by Sergeant Matlovich and Ensign Berg when the military dismissed them dishonorably. And I learned of organizations like The National Gay Task Force, elated to know that we could exercise some power. I was buoyed by the courage of these people, they were the positive role models I had long searched for. Their brave stands fed my emerging self-love, and helped me to lay the foundation of what would unfold as a quite militant future.

In the beginning I tried to share my discoveries with Jason. I would repeat excitedly to him the study done on homosexuality in sports, citing how many professional quarterbacks were like us. He would turn a deaf ear. Sometimes he would react angrily. He refused to face the issue. I was coming to see myself not as homosexual but as gay. He hated the word. I had stopped dating girls altogether. He was going steady with a pretty blonde. We were moving in opposite directions, though still coming together for a common need. Many times I could not help but loathe him. But then I would find myself in his Mustang, his hand would brush my crotch and our world would be well again.

It was soon after I encountered Don that I began to pull away from Jason. Don's face, my daydreams about it, made me realize that I wanted much more than Jason would give me. I wanted love. And having begun to accept myself as a gay person, I was ready to reclaim something I had lost along the way: my Indian heritage. I had come full circle. The pain of my experience with racial hatred had made me stronger as a gay person. What I suffered silently once I would not suffer a second time. Now my love of myself as a gay man was peeling away the layers of self-hatred the world had coated me with as a child. The Indian in me was struggling to get out. The reclamation would be slow. Years later I would meet other gay Indians and begin to integrate the gay and ethnic facets of my personality. But I had taken the first step.

Reaching inside for my ethnicity, I found myself unable to make allowances for Jason's bigotry. Each time I heard him make some racist remark during the day, I would challenge him over it at night. Predictably, an argument would ensue. He would threaten to break our connection but would never follow through. Why should he? He had a lover and a girlfriend, all he wanted. In the end it was I who told him one night that the sex we shared was not enough. He did not protest. That would have insinuated that our relationship meant something to him. It was the end of February. That night we had sex for the last time.

For the remainder of that year Jason was to become devoted to the girlfriend he had neglected for me. He even embraced the religion he had ridiculed in the past. Neither one of us tried to reestablish the bond. We did not speak again, and in the classes we shared it was as if the other did not exist. Years later a friend mentioned to me that Jason was in jail. He had been implicated in a murder-for-hire scheme and was under psychiatric observation.

After my break from Jason I found myself even more preoccupied with Don. Ours was a love affair of the eyes, the safest, most haunting sort of romance. We would pass each other daily on the way to class. Always our eyes would lock. In his eyes burned a sad hope, one that must surely have been reflected in mine. Our eyes would linger on one another a moment longer than prudent, then we would turn away as if suddenly conscious of the world around us. Across the expanse of the library we would gaze at one another, smiling sheepishly on being caught. But we never exchanged a word. There was so much we could have shared had we had a little more courage, had the world around us been less threatening. But we didn't have the strength, and time slipped away from my leopard and me. Over the years I would rarely think of Jason, with whom I shared so much pleasure. Don's face I could not forget. Seven years after I last saw him I wrote a poem, the last four lines of which echo a question that still tugs at me:

> I wonder today where you might be.
> Have the passing years set your heart free?
> Do you think of how we touched?
> Ruled by fear, we missed so much.

▼

John J. Carr

San Francisco, California

Closets Are Not For Living In:

a gay senior's story

The term "coming out", as it is presently used in our community, would have meant nothing to most of my generation when we were young. There are now almost as many meanings to the term as there are gay people. Since breaking through these painful barriers fairly late in my life, I have found that coming out is not necessarily a one-time process, and that it contains great potential for individual growth, limited only by an individual's willingness to participate.

As a community, we have developed a variety of support systems which have been generated by our own needs as gays and lesbians. Two of these support systems have made the difference for me. The first, the gay group of Alcoholics Anonymous, helped me to get back in control of my life. They not only showed me the way to a life free of alcohol, but also validated me as a gay person. The second was Dignity, an association of lesbian and gay Roman Catholics, which enhanced this process by teaching me, in a way that was not based on an archaic theology, that gay people had a spiritual side to their beings which could be developed in accordance with their needs. I will always be profoundly grateful to both groups, as well as to many in the larger gay community who have played an important role in my own self-acceptance.

I was born in Chicago in August 1920, and all but grew up inside the doors of the beautiful Servite Church of Our Lady of Sorrows on Chicago's West Side, where my parents had been married. When I graduated from a Catholic grammar school, I immediately entered the preparatory novitiate of a monastic order where I remained for three years. I cannot conceive of any way in which my upbringing could have been more strongly influenced by the proscriptive doctrines of Roman Catholicism. My mother passed away when I was ten years old and, along with my younger sister, I was given over to the care of my father's aunt, already seventy years old. She died when I was sixteen. My relationship with my father, never a quality one, went into a steady decline from which it never fully recovered.

During those years I unconsciously internalized homophobia along with the rest of society, and this became one of my survival techniques. The economic climate created by the Great Depression, among other things, put the possibilities of higher education beyond my reach. As my father had never provided for me in any meaningful way, and since I left the Carmelite Order on my great aunt's passing, I became acutely aware that there were no options open to me except to join the work force. I found a job on the railroad.

Shortly after Pearl Harbor, I enlisted in the Navy at the age of twenty-one. I was sent to the Naval Training Station at San Diego for indoctrination and training. Shortly after getting out of "boot camp" I sought out the Roman Catholic chaplain to try to reconcile my erotic attraction to other men with what I had been taught by the Church. My experience with Roman Catholic clergy up to that time had provided me with a sense of assurance that what I was relating to a priest, in or out of the confessional, was being treated as confidential. My "confidential" disclosures to the Chaplain became the basis for my separation from the service. The armed forces could not tolerate queers. We were not even accorded the privilege of confidentiality with our own clergy!

I received an honorable discharge, but this was small consolation. My trust had been violated by someone I had been brought up to believe could be trusted. I was hurt and confused. After being discharged in San Diego, I returned to Chicago, lonelier than I have ever been at any time during my life. Money was not a problem, at least in the short-term. I had enough to keep me going until I went back to work. I had been on military leave from the railroad, and I was assured by law of reinstatement. What I needed most I did not have: someone I could trust and to whom I could reach out in this time of emotional need. Life was not simplified by the fact that I was now in the minority of twenty-two-year-olds who were not in military uniforms during wartime. One small ray of sunshine in all of this was that my Selective Service classification reverted to 1-C which indicated that I had served honorably and had been discharged, rather than 4-F, the classification of those who were totally rejected for whatever reasons.

I returned to work for the railroad company by which I had been employed prior to entering military service. During this time, in the early 1940s, I learned about an area at the Illinois Central Railroad Station in Chicago which today we would call a "cruising" area. Even though I was doing nothing illegal, my continuing presence there provided an opportunity for a criminal, who identified himself as a plainclothes policeman, to prey on my fear by frightening me into showing him my railroad I.D., along with a savings passbook on a Chicago bank. Armed with the knowledge that I had a small amount of money in one of the banks, this individual made thinly veiled "suggestions" that there might be a way to keep my employer from finding out. It is not beyond the realm of possibility that this person was in fact a member of the Chicago Police Department. The fact is that I had been victimized by a blackmailer to the tune of about three hundred dollars, a considerable sum in those days. It was all I had, but I was too terrified to try to do anything about it, if indeed the authorities would have done anything anyway. I was not the type of citizen who warranted assistance.

The experience with the blackmailer terrified me more than I realized at the time, and this unpleasant memory only served to increase my paranoia and fear of being discovered by "big-brother" or some other ghostly disciplinary authority. For these reasons I chose the relative safety and security of anonymity over the risks of exposure and the calamities that would follow if I had tried to identify myself in any way. I was fearful of going into the bars which were the center of what social life there was for us. Consequently, I never had the opportunity, in any realistic sense, of becoming part of whatever social groups there may have been. The forerunner of today's gay bars, known as "queer joints," were few and far between, and the ones which did survive usually were in back alleys or other unsavory locations in the larger cities. Even then, a patron's peace of mind in such a place was usually in direct proportion to the "insurance" payments made by the bar's proprietor to the police department. Police raids on queer joints were not uncommon, with the patrons herded into the black mariah and off to the slammer, and often to exposure, loss of employment, loss of reputation, and sometimes to ultimate breakdown and suicide. This at least was one indignity which I was spared, but for the remainder of my stay in the Midwest, I burrowed ever more deeply into my subterranean cave, keeping my true identity hidden and trying to make the best of a bad bargain.

In 1945 I decided to leave the Midwest and to return to California. Even though I had a good position with the railroad as a private secretary in their general offices in Cleveland, there was too much about my experiences which were depressing me. While I was on the West Coast during my brief naval experience, I became aware that life in the West was somewhat less oppressive for homosexuals than it had been in the Midwest. San Francisco, particularly, was more tolerant than any other place I had been, even though it was not the mecca for gay and lesbian people that it has now become. I decided to move to San Francisco, where I immediately embarked on a thirty-year career as a seafarer aboard merchant ships.

At some point during my seafaring career, I crossed the fine line between recreational, social drinking and pathological, excessive drinking. I became a full-blown alcoholic. Even though it is over nineteen years since I have taken a drink, I have not forgotten the nightmarish horror of alcohol addiction. My initial association with the only gay group of Alcoholics Anonymous in San Francisco, if not in the entire country, was the beginning of my open association with the gay community in 1969 at the age of forty-nine. In addition to helping me with my drinking problem, they also taught me about something that I had forgotten even existed: real love and caring. This association with the gay community conferred on me a sense of belonging that I had never before experienced. For the first time I felt the freedom to be who I was, and I was no longer willing to try to be someone I was not.

In much the same way that I was accepted by Gay A.A., I was also welcomed into Dignity. They taught me to be who I am, and that I cannot be what some other person or institution thinks I should be. The gay or lesbian Catholic is involved in a two-front battle: with the Church because we are gay, and with the gay community because we are Catholic and fight tenaciously to remain so, in spite of the Church's continuing oppression. For my own part, this institution stripped me of my integrity once — it will never do so again.

Because of the support I have received from Gay A.A. and Dignity, I have regained my own sense of integrity and am proud to be a gay senior, slowing down perhaps, but not yet ready to withdraw from the fight for our rights. It is a real joy to know that my retirement years do not have to be spent in hiding as my formative years were.

Ready for new challenges, I applied for admission as an undergraduate and pursued a program in philosophy. I continued on a graduate level and received a Master of Arts degree from San Francisco State University at the age of sixty-two. I am starting on my second Master's program now.

The few noisy queers at Stonewall have multiplied beyond anyone's most optimistic expectations, and we proclaim to the world that we are here to stay. The AIDS epidemic and its predictable homophobic backlashes have bonded us ever more closely, as we support and care for those in our community who are suffering. We have been hurt before, and will be again, but we will never return to the subterranean caves of yesteryear.

I do not regret my past, for I believe I have done the best I could with the tools I had. But as someone who has spent much of his life in a tributary to the mainstream, knowing that I now *belong* to a community for which I care deeply — and which cares for me in return — has made the long wait worth it. Whenever the Supreme Navigator orders this old sailor to weigh anchor and cast off for the final voyage, it will be with the feeling that it has *all* been worthwhile.

Mark Kruger
West Hollywood, California

Managing the Team

The process of coming out for me was twofold: my social initiation and my sexual one. The two were separated by more than seven years.

I came out socially on the eve of 1978 at the age of twenty-one. From that night forward I began to accept my sexual identity and allowed myself to be seen — with steadily growing pride — in gay places and with other persons of my special orientation.

The bars, dancing, dating, discos — all were extraordinary, enlightening experiences. Lately, however, I reflect more often on my sexual coming out which, at barely fourteen years of age, was truly a revelation.

As long as I can remember I have sensed something special about guys. There was a thrill, a rush, a high — nothing I could put into words at the time. But in one incredible moment, I knew what to do about it.

In the predominantly rural states of the Great Plains where I grew up, a town with a population of 20,000 is a real city. My city had a large public high school with a surprisingly diverse, well-rounded curriculum, where a student gifted in the arts could be assured of finding like-minded nonconformists. However, I was raised Catholic, although only marginally devout, and had already attended parochial school for eight years by the time I entered my freshman year at the only private high school in town.

Our school was substantially smaller than the public school, a "poor relation" in many respects. One result of this status was that boys were deemed worthy of notice only by achieving a measure of accomplishment on the athletic battlefield. And our boys generally met the challenge admirably, often excelling in regional and statewide competitions in various sports.

All but a few of us, that is. I was scrawny, shy, and self-conscious — pegged long before as an easy object of scorn by my peers. I was bright and artistically talented, which was bad enough at that age, but I was also widely considered a "sissy."

Surely most of the kids had no idea of the complex implications of that label; it was applied to me principally because of my complete incompetence at all things athletic. I was certain no one could possibly have discerned my secret fascination with guys.

Though I had no real "hands-on" sexual experience, I had discovered as early as the seventh grade that I was light years ahead of most of my peers in terms of sexual maturity. That was the year my mother had explained the facts of life. I had also read *Everything You Always Wanted to Know About Sex (But Were Afraid to Ask)*, and had heard the toughest punk in class telling his pals how he had just discovered the thrill of masturbation. I had been doing it religiously for two years.

My reputation for being soft meant that my self-esteem and confidence were nil, but I weathered the constant razzing in embarrassed silence and hoped that life would someday get better. I felt like the nothing I seemed to be to the rest of humanity. Yet, though I could not be a jock, I reasoned that I could reduce the taunting if I earned an athletic letter on my school jacket. I signed on as student manager of the track and wrestling teams.

A student manager is charged with maintaining equipment, recording statistics, taping sore ankles, distributing towels, straightening up the locker room, and other similarly fascinating tasks, all of which I abhorred. But there was one fringe benefit which made it all wonderfully worthwhile: I got to see all those grand young men in all their naked glory!

Corey was my co-manager, and though we had been classmates for years, we had never really been friends. Corey was a misfit of a different sort. He seemed to have no outstanding qualities whatsoever — a nice enough guy, but average in every way. To this day, I don't know whether Corey is gay; I rather doubt it. But in the ninth grade, he became a catalyst for the development of much of who I am.

While the teams practiced, Corey and I hung out in the locker room playing cards, and discussing the relative merits of the team members' bodies. Frankly, I do not remember how the subject first came up. But Corey was entering puberty at that time as well, so I imagine the subject of sex of any persuasion was tantalizing.

It wasn't long before we had to try some of the things we had been fantasizing about. After practice one day, I went with Corey to his house. At the far corner of the backyard was a small storage shed — dark, damp, and empty except for an ancient lawnmower, other miscellaneous gardening tools, and a beat-up bicycle with two flat tires and no seat.

No discussion was necessary; we both knew what to do. Afraid to undress completely in case we had to hide in a hurry, we both pulled our jeans and shorts around our ankles. Unable to see a thing, I laid face down on the cold concrete slab and waited. I heard Corey spit and then felt pressure at my asshole. Slowly, and surprisingly painlessly, he entered me.

I guess I was lucky that Corey was not hung very big, but from the first thrusts in and out of me, I knew this was what I was meant for: to serve, to provide pleasure to other men, which in turn was pleasure for me. I felt so happy, so fulfilled!

And so afraid — afraid that what had happened could be perceived by anyone who looked at me. I felt somehow marked, like the badge of adultery Hester Prynne had to wear in *The Scarlet Letter*, which my freshman English class had read that year.

But from that moment, despite the fear, I could not get enough. Corey apparently agreed, for we did it every chance we could. I tried fucking him a few times too, but didn't enjoy it very much.

We developed a new game while passing time in the locker room: instead of playing poker for money, we played for "service time." That is, the loser of each game owed five minutes of sexual gratification to the other – mouth or ass, according to the winner's choice. I dared not make it too obvious, but I deliberately lost nearly every time, marvelling all the while at my consistent bad luck and secretly wishing I could pay my "debt" to a dozen or so of my favorite members of the team.

I never did get up the nerve to offer my services to any other boys at school, and Corey and I drifted apart again by the end of the school year. Once again, my only outlet became jacking off, which I did every night while fantasizing about how I could please the athletes. I still think of some of them and wonder what might have happened if I had been a bit more bold.

Tommy Thunder*
Long Island, New York

The Trench

Staring up at the luminous green of an oscilloscope, I gently turn the control knob of the blood pressure monitor, calibrating its signal for the last time. The jagged, wavering lines darting across the screen show a racing pulse and sagging pressure in the veins and arteries of my patient. In this inner sanctum of flashing lights and screeching alarms, the ebb and flow of life is measured by the steady drip of the intravenous line, by the slow moaning hiss of the respirator.

I solemnly watch the rise and fall of a young man's chest as oxygen-enriched air is blown into lungs rendered useless by pneumocystis carinii pneumonia. Reaching over the bedrail, I tighten the bandages covering the catheter in his wrist, first pushing aside tangles of clear plastic tubing hanging like tentacles from the pocked ceiling. For scores of men and women in the withering finale of AIDS, this crowded cubicle is their final vision. They soon succumb to the inevitable coma and respiratory arrest.

In this cursed Coliseum of the 1980s, life and death joust in the arena of medical technology. The endotracheal tubes, beeping pumps, and panicked monitors are faltering weapons against a silent and lethal enemy. That is the isolation room of the intensive care unit, a place the belabored nurses and techs call "the trench."

A black female heroin addict lay on this same bed months before, her eyes wide with fear, rolling her head from side to side on a sweaty pillow. Under arduous breaths, she implored "save me Jesus, please save me sweet Jesus," while the chains shackling her to the frame rattled in mocking retort. Outside the room, a sullen prison guard flipped the pages of a crumpled newspaper, waiting out the hours until his charge died. A jovial morgue attendant later wheeled the body away in a squeaky, cloth-shrouded gurney. Little time passed before the next victim of this dreaded disease arrived. Here there is no sweet Jesus, no miracles, no mercy. Death reigns as supreme champion.

One need not search through pages of obscure scripture to envision hell. For gay men of this decade, the inferno is frightfully real, camouflaged in the bleach-scrubbed neatness of the isolation room. The borders of this no-man's land, marked by flags warning "blood and body fluid precautions," encircle a battlefield where others have fled the siege to the safety of their ignorance and prejudice.

I silently witness the deaths of gay men from my bleak vantage point, their gaunt faces and hollow eyes peering from the darkest corners of my memories. Hidden behind a mask of unequivocally "straight" mannerisms and a heavily muscled frame, I am a foot soldier in this biological blitzkrieg, braving the strafing of viral bullets, homophobic graffiti smeared on the walls, and the muffled grumblings of "queer" and "faggot" from coworkers.

In this fetid outpost, I have served four years as a medical technician in a Long Island hospital. In this unrelenting and hostile environment, the illusions of my beliefs were ground into the dust. Within the confines of the isolation room, my fragile dignity was tempered in the flames of plague. Despite the endless parade of human misery marching before my stoic eyes, I chose to remain behind enemy lines, plodding through a landscape of lost minds and broken bodies. In the face of private holocaust, I had to reach within to find new strength to persevere, to survive until this disease surrenders to cure.

Finding escape in the serenity of the barbell, my muscles

grew thick and hard under the crush of clanging plates. Toughened by the discipline of the karate dojo, I explored the depths of my courage and endurance. Rising from the ashes of the trench, my new soul would fly free like an iron phoenix.

Panic burned in the pit of my stomach. The quiet practice of breath control I gleaned from the martial arts failed to soothe my troubled spirit. I was losing the war of nerves, my cool composure and professional detachment not enough to stem the rising tide of fear.

The torments of the bronchoscopy room stabbed to the core of my well-rehearsed indifference. His close-cropped hair, slender limbs, and gentle voice could not disguise the cloudy spots of the chest X-ray. Helping him onto the green sheets of a flouroscopy table, I glanced at dark purple welts rising between the pale cheeks of his buttocks. A crammed scribble in the hospital chart revealed all: "thirty-four-year-old white male homosexual, history of herpes proctitis." The following line – "rule out pneumocystis, rule out AIDS" – sent the physicians and techs scurrying behind barriers of double surgical gloves, double gown, double masks, foot covers, goggles, and hoods.

He whined and gagged as the slender neck of the bronchoscope, black and slick with lubricant, slithered down his throat, deep into the ravaged recesses of his lungs. Long biopsy cables were then threaded through the scope. At the end of the cable, miniature steel jaws bit into the soft tissue. Small gray plugs of lung were flushed into sterile specimen jars containing formaldehyde, alcohol or saline solution. Holding the jar in my gloved hand, I brought its contents into the harsh glare of an examination lamp. A gentle twist of the wrist sent the tiny orbs racing through the preservative solution, like devil planets bumping and crashing in a universe gone mad.

The AIDS barrage finally reached home. That young man in the bronchoscopy room was nearly my age, of the same Italian descent, and lived only blocks away from me. The bombs fell close; no blaring headline or troubled television report could compare to the brutal education of the trench.

Caring for the sick and dying at the hospital by day, I played a calm masquerade. Dressed in white uniform, I mouthed the same trite words as the doctors and nurses, and wore the same blank face which blunted the calamilty we faced every day. At night the perimeters of my emotional bunker fell. Stark visions invaded my sleep and trampled on my dreams. Trapped in the labyrinth of the isolation room, my matted hair pressed against the stained sheets anointed with blood and bile. Comatose eyes, taped shut to prevent dehydration, were blind to the frothy saliva rolling down my cheek, my throat violated by an endotracheal tube. Surely this was to be my fate. Had I not "sinned" as lustily as my dying patients?

We tumbled, breathless and laughing, onto the cool, autumn ground, our young bodies pleasantly tired from playing football. Standing behind my best friend, I reveled in the warmth and happiness that surrounded our group of buddies, despite the chill of a late afternoon and the frosty breezes that reddened our cheeks and tossed dry leaves.

I leaned forward, and in a second of pure trust and innocence kissed him on the top of his head. At the time, it seemed the natural thing to do, being deliriously happy in the bonds of male camaraderie, so at home in the company of boys my age. The sudden uproar, the startled commotion in the group surprised and confused me. I had done something terribly wrong, crossed the boundary of some unwritten law that I did not understand.

They called me "queer." What did this mean? At once confused and afraid, I blushed and meekly stammered that the kiss was an accident, that I didn't mean to do it. *No, no . . . please don't call me a "queer,"* I thought. Could I not run and catch, could I not tackle and laugh and shout like everyone else?

From that very moment, all the lies began. The kiss was no accident, nor my innocent enjoyment of it. Whatever this difference was, deep inside I knew it had to remain buried, hidden from the notice of my parents, the blind date at the high school dance, the college girlfriend, the priests and brothers who taught me, and the social workers and counselors who tried to define my anxiety.

Many years passed before I realized my true identity, daring to define myself as "gay." The actual moment when this wave of quivering passion rolled over me, forever changing my life, is as clear to me as that innocent kiss of my boyhood. Running my hands over the taut back muscles of a teen-aged co-worker, surrounded by bubbling vats of chemicals in a Queens metal plating shop, I surrendered to the sweet fragrance of his tender skin, the fine mist of sweat that caressed his shoulders, the lean knots of muscle that ran down to his hips. He loved my backrubs, and I yearned to oblige him, thrilled to the core by the touch of another man, enthralled by the voltage that coursed through me as my hips pressed against the tight blue jeans that hugged his butt.

Ironically, we never had sex . Yet through him, in the briefest moments of touch, I discovered a swirling sea of hidden emotion. Like Prometheus, I dared to steal carnal flames only vaguely understood, even dangerous to possess. An undisciplined puppy, suddenly breaking free of my leash, I ran wild, unaware of the perils in the woods.

I discovered the bars, the discos, the bath houses. I succumbed to the illusion of a sexual culture that confused love and true freedom with decadence and promiscuity. It was the only game in town, the only one I knew existed. Even today, I remain bitter and resentful at being so easily deceived, so willing to mistake "more" for "better," chained to a false ethic that equated my sexiness and desirability with the number of men I bedded.

Perhaps, I was one of the luckier puppies in the woods. An unseen and benevolent hand grabbed me by the scruff of the neck, slapped my backside, and chided me for running away from the master.

"No my little one, you are not like the others. You are not even a puppy! You are the wolf of sinew, claw, and fang. Your home is on the high rocks, with the eagles, not here. Silly little one, did you not hear the ants coming?"

And yes, the silent army of ants did invade the dark forest. Their poisoned jaws stripped away the flowers and foliage, consumed the unaware, and left a barren land in their wake.

Destiny forced me to bear a heavy burden of doubt, guilt, and grinding fear. In the confusion of the early years of the AIDS epidemic, the most disturbing aspect was a dismal lack of scientific knowledge of the disease. Many hospitals and health care personnel suddenly confronted a pathogen without a name or known mode of transmission. The situation was made worse by a stifling atmosphere of homophobia on all levels of the hospital hierarchy, from dullard porter scribbling obscenities on the elevator walls to the private snickerings of some physicians.

The darkest hours of my personal crisis came on an afternoon in April 1985. The media buzzed over the promise of a new antibody blood test that indicated exposure to the recently isolated AIDS virus. Medical authorities warned of the test's drawbacks, but that mattered little to me then. Compelled to learn the truth of my own health, giving a vial of blood seemed to be the logical means of reaching ultimate decisions.

Too many times I silently endured the sad look of numb hopelessness on the faces of visitors in the intensive care unit. Their tears and pleas to get well were answered by slow decline and death. I resolved never to burden family and friends with a lingering decay of mind and body. Taking my own life would be infinitely preferable to rotting in the isolation room.

My tattered sanity, surviving on the rigid discipline of the karate dojo, braced by years of sweat and grunt in the gym, reached the breaking point. With the appearance of the first lesion, the first telltale symptom, I was prepared to die.

Slowly, and with great dignity, I seated myself on a bamboo mat, in the respectful *seiza* posture, with knees and toes touching the ground and body resting on the heels. Facing the silkscreen backdrop of the shrine, I meditated on its cool watercolors. Ancient warriors galloped across the panels, their lances and broadswords brandished in the air seconds before the clash of horse and armor.

The blood-red shimmer of a votive candle played over the gleaming steel of my *wakizashi* short sword, the razor edge capturing and refracting the crimson light like a precious stone. Thin wisps of incense floated past sedate bonsai trees into the alcove of my room. Reverently lifting the blade from the mat, I wrapped a clean white cloth around it, covering half the cutting edge. Clutching it with chilled and sweaty hands, I placed the tapered point against the soft white skin of my abdomen. In macabre rehearsal, I drew the sword from left to right, leaving a long thin scratch.

To the side of the sand-colored futon, a 50 cc. syringe waited in a bottom drawer. A four-inch spinal needle jutted from the tip like a bayonet, ready to force air into my vein, and deliver a quick release. Placing the blade down, I paused a few seconds to steel my nerves.

After four slow weeks that felt like four centuries, the results of my blood test arrived at the office of a private physician in Manhattan. Lifting the phone to my ear, I dialed the numbers, at times pausing to deeply inhale. The words charged through me, striking so fast their meaning was briefly lost in the maelstrom of my thoughts. I stammered a "thank you" and gently hung up the phone.

A calm breeze danced over the wind chimes, their sweet metallic notes piercing the silence like the cry of a nightbird in the green forest. Fear slowly faded with each deep, deliberate breath. I slid the oiled blade back into its lacquered scabbard, and returned the weapon to the black wooden stand. Wiping away my tears, I bowed forward, placing my face and hands on the bamboo mat. Then I stood up, smoothing out the wrinkles of my *gi*, and cinching in the belt around my waist. I drew open the blinds, letting in the blazing light of an afternoon sun. The shrine was bathed in fiery orange hue, and the sword was baptized in a golden aura of new life.

Sinking deeper into a wide "horse stance," the sinews in my thighs quivered slightly as I struggled to keep my balance. Damp gray fog rose from the chilled lake, making the mossy rocks slick, and footing deceptive. Inhaling deep into my abdomen, imaginary roots sprang from the soles of my black kung-fu slippers into the stone precipice. My feet clasped the cold stone like talons, as I perched thirty feet above the rubble-lined shore. One slip, one moment of doubt, would send me plummeting down. The sleeves of my *gi* whipped and snapped as I punched into the morning air, each blow accented with a gruff burst of air from my chest. I delivered the last thrust at full speed and power, with a booming "kiai" shout that reverberated over the placid water.

Along the shores of this lake, nestled in the pine-scented wilderness of the Adirondacks, I found refuge. Each year a group of my friends and I don boots and backpack and retreat to the peace and seclusion of the woods for a few days. We welcome the relief from the pressures of job and daily life. For me, the isolated campsite became a training ground to sharpen my martial skills. While my buddies doze or lazily canoe across the lake, I find happiness in the bush, flinging sharp metal stars at the trees, or slicing branches in two with the sword.

"Coming out" to my backwoods buddies meant more than saying I was homosexual. They had known about that for years. Here in the forest, I found a stage to uncover a hidden personality. A different man stepped into my skin from the moment that fateful phone call inaugurated my new beginning. Perhaps I had inherited the soul of the "gay" man history prefers to forget — the fierce samurai, or the proud athlete of ancient Greece.

I thirsted for excitement and adventure, to challenge flesh and spirit to reach new heights. At the gym, intoxicated by the scent of sweat and liniment, I flexed and grimaced under bar-bending weights, soon breaking all my personal records. Strength and courage became my cardinal virtues, survival my password. When so many others had been robbed of life and health, I cherished these visceral moments to the fullest. The body count at the hospital hardened me to death and suffering. The nightmares disappeared eventually, but I found I could no longer shed tears at funerals. What did not kill me only made me stronger.

This summer I merged with my fantasy, forging ideal into action. It was time to reveal the final transformation.

Stepping from the lean-to, I tightened my ammo belt around my waist, and folded up the brim of my boonie hat, commando-style. Small twigs crackled beneath heavy black combat boots as I strode down to the shore. My friends, busily preparing the sleek aluminum canoe, seemed stunned for a moment, confronted by the camouflage battle dress uniform, and the canvas case slung over my shoulder. Gone was the bar-hopping bathhouse boy of the seventies. In his place now stood a living anachronism of bushido and barbell, far to the right of "butch" in the homosexual spectrum. A new breed had arrived, untainted by society's expectations of femininity or phony macho.

We paddled to the far end of the lake, greeted by the roar and hiss of the waterfall. As I walked over the wooden bridge straddling the foaming, turbulent water below, I paused to reflect on the power of the rushing currents, to which even the hardest stone must eventually yield. We trudged inland through damp foliage until finding a clearing deep in the woods. My friends gathered around, anticipating the opening of the mysterious canvas sack.

I unzipped the case from top to bottom, spreading the flaps wide open to reveal the bulging contents. Easing the assault rifle from the case, I admired the sculpted barrel, its hard black steel shining with a thin layer of oil. Grasping the folding stock tucked along the side, I pulled it out and back. With the click of a steel locking pin, the rifle grew to full length.

Looking over at my astonished friends, I smiled as I ran my hand over the gun's smooth brown wood. Reaching into my pocket, I produced a long black magazine, swollen with thirty rounds of hollow point ammunition. I slid the clip into place, pushing it deeply into the receptacle. The magazine hung down ominously from the smooth belly of the stock.

I pinned a paper silhouette to a stout tree, then paced back to firing position. With a quick stroke of my hand against the slide handle, the cocked weapon was ready for action. The rifle roared into life, a hot tongue of blue-white flame erupting from the barrel. My ears rang from the concussion of the blast, as the weapon jerked and quivered in my grip. An empty cartridge case spurted from the action, flying in an upward arc and then falling onto the damp leaves. We stood in shocked silence for some seconds as the echo ricocheted across the mountains.

In the corridors of my fantasy, the mortally wounded paper figure suddenly came to life, as if cold purple blood coursed through its veins. The screaming shadow charged straight at me, holding aloft his handcuffs and holy book. I can see his livid face, rabid foam running from his jowls. The evil juggernaut rushed over the battlefield, mindless of the bodies strewn in his path. A quick mutation, and like a chameleon he changed into a jack-booted fascist, shrouded in neatly pressed uniform. Still, he charged ever closer.

The assault rifle cut the air with the staccato rhythm of rapid fire, my gun blowing lead in hot response to the urgings of my trigger finger. The rounds bore into his viral torso, shattering the skull insignia on his chest. For a second, the impact sent spastic shudders through his limbs. Shock and disbelief contorted his face, as he was staggered by the abrupt reprisal. The bloated corpse stumbled and fell to the mud.

Off in the distance, the dawn's light shone through flame and smoke rising from the destroyed camp. Abandoned watchtowers stared down at empty shackles and smoldering rubble. Climbing from the trench, I kicked mud from my combat boots and strode over fallen barbed wire into freedom.

Guy-Oriedo Weston

Stratford, New Jersey

Crossing Bridges

One Sunday afternoon in the spring of '83, a friend and I arrived in Philadelphia from our insulated suburban communities in search of some sort of gay social activity. As we drove through Center City, we noticed dark lavender newspaper boxes on several corners with *Gay News* written on them. "Maybe we can find something in the *Gay News*," I told my friend. But both of us were afraid to be seen buying a gay newspaper in broad daylight. We argued and eventually flipped a coin. I lost. As inconspicuously as possible, I approached the box, dropped in my three quarters, took the paper and walked back to my car, hoping that I had not been noticed.

That was three years ago...

This past summer I befriended a visitor from Latin America who was so excited by the freedom of expression that he witnessed among gay men in Greenwich Village that he could not wait to try it himself. One evening as we walked down a residential street in downtown Philadelphia, he took my hand and held it. I did not know whether to hold his hand or not. As we walked down the street I thought: *Four months ago I moved from suburbia to "gay" down-*

town Philly. I have a "gay" job, working for the city's AIDS Control Program. I write for the gay press and spend very little time projecting conventional heterosexual masculinity for the sake of peers, co-workers, or family, who are too narrow-minded to accept who I really am. I am not going to get fired from my job if I am "discovered." Is there any reason to be afraid to be myself? NO! I put my thoughts aside, braced myself, and continued to walk along talking to my friend: with one eye scanning in front of us waiting for a homophobe to hurl a brick or yell faggot. The first few blocks were pretty empty but we eventually reached South Street, an avante garde social gathering place full of restaurants, shops, and people who stay around until well after midnight.

Although South Street is the one place in Philly where anything goes, I was slightly apprehensive because there were so many people around. Surprisingly, nobody seemed to notice us. A couple of people snickered or said things under their breath, but no one gave us any reason to feel the least bit intimidated. The most noticeable reaction came from a gay friend of mine who did a doubletake and looked after us in disbelief as we walked by the restaurant where he worked.

The next day, out of sheer curiosity, I decided that we would walk down Chestnut Street, a main thoroughfare in the business district of the city. It was about noon and the sidewalks were full of people from the surrounding stores and offices on their lunch breaks. Again we failed to elicit any overt expressions of disgust and the majority of people seemed not to notice us, although we did get a few more stares and one or two verbal insults that were not loud enough to warrant any concern.

This experience caused me to re-examine my values, but not to the extent that I considered constantly flaunting my sexual orientation to see how much I could get away with. If I continued to parade proudly down Chestnut Street, eventually some belligerent anti-gay behavior would cross my path and I do not want to walk around wondering when it's going to occur.

On the other hand, I no longer consider it necessary to keep the real me a prisoner inside myself. I don't have to be selectively invisible, or take great pains to conceal my identity for fear that the wrong person might find out. I can just be myself. If someone asks, I'll tell them. But I don't have to announce it to everyone that comes by, anymore than I announce anything else about myself.

My attraction for men goes back almost as far as I can remember. When I was four years old an older boy threatened to take me and four of my playmates into his bathroom individually to search our pants to see if we had stolen a lost toy. I was disappointed because my turn never came. There was something exciting about the prospect of that older boy going into my pants. By the time I was seven I was going into a neighbor's garage for he and I to compare penises and poke them against each other. When I was ten I attempted anal sex with another boy for the first time. At thirteen, I had my first ejaculation and realized soon thereafter that this same-sex attraction was not just a passing thing. I would have to work hard to become "normal." I had five sex partners throughout childhood and early adolescence. Although these sexual experiences had been infrequent, I knew what I wanted and thought it was wrong. Since my father was in the Air Force, I was spending most of my free time in children's activities at the local Protestant chapel set up for military personnel and their families. It was very clear to me that God wanted me to be an all-American, patriotic, macho, sexist Christian little boy. And I knew that he would make me just that, if I would deny myself and follow *Him*.

My father's career took me away from my last sex partner and friend. For the rest of my adolescence, I remained celibate while I attempted to rid myself of this "deviant sexual orientation."

Following the faith of my upbringing, I chose to attend a middle-of-the-road Christian liberal arts college after high school. Even though no one at the college knew my secret, I was encouraged to feel guilty and seek change, because of the negative depictions of homosexuality in Bible study and in adolescent psychology class.

During this time a movement which called itself Radical Evangelical was getting a lot of publicity in Christian magazines. This school of thought was known for an unusual preoccupation with social issues.

One of the issues that they were "radical" about was a "new" look at homosexuality and the scriptures. Frequently, they were less judgemental and some were even supportive and offered resources such as psychological support to persons such as myself. Initially, I was slightly suspicious of this movement's outlook on homosexuality because it contradicted my literalist interpretation of the Bible. Eventually I became excited by this new perspective and involved myself in other "unpopular" causes they advocated. With a similar concern about issues such as U.S. involvement in Central America, I decided to finish my undergraduate work at a theological seminary in Costa Rica.

While Costa Rica is accurately reputed to be the most peaceful democratic nation in Latin America, it is surrounded by political turmoil resulting primarily from its northern border with Nicaragua. It was rewarding to be involved in a Christian movement that saw its mission as helping to put an end to the blatant exploitation of a people by Nicaragua's Anastasio Somoza Debayle: the ruthless dictator that looted his country before being overthrown by the Sandinistas. It was evident, though, that people fighting to achieve the most basic tenets of "life, liberty and the pursuit of happiness" would not get around to dealing with an issue such as homosexuality. As a gay friend of mine from Nicaragua once put it: "there will never be a gay liberation movement here as long as people are fighting for their lives."

Of course, the absence of a visible gay movement did not mean that there were any fewer gay people around. By a stroke of luck, my roommate at the seminary was gay. Unfortunately, our fun did not last for long and eventually we stopped being friends. "God would get us if we didn't quit it," as far as he was concerned.

I knew better. After having tried to fight off my passions for several years and having learned to read the Bible in a different light, I had concluded that God created me as I am; that my sexual orientation was normal and that I could love a man without feeling guilty. Since my roommate thought such words were blasphemous, I decided to leave him alone.

Frustrated and lonely, I decided to resort to the popular cruising area in the central park. The equivalent of less than five dollars bought me a friendly hustler and another two dollars and thirty-five cents paid for a hotel room in the *Zona Roja*, the Red Zone, for a few hours. Eventually I made two regular "friends" who despised each other because I paid such good money and I would only see one of them per day. If I'd had any sense I would have "passed," allowing my friends to think that I was a black Latin American, instead of telling them that I was North American. Then I would have only had to pay about two dollars and fifty cents for tricks, instead of the "expensive" five dollar rate for American visitors.

This was fun for about two months. Eventually, I could not stand it anymore. I had always wanted to live out my sexual life the same way that "conventional" couples do — in a covenant relationship, according to my religious convictions. My hustler friends and I had actually become great buddies, but they were still seventy-five percent money-motivated.

Feeling distracted from school, I returned to the United States to work out the struggles of my sexual orientation with the intention of returning to Latin America as soon as I got myself together.

Soon after returning to this country, I began to seek out some of the gay religious groups I had heard about previously. After my first meeting I followed most of the members into the gay bar next door. I was appalled. I could not shift gears so quickly. The brand of Christianity that I came to know as a child would never permit that the after-church social be held in a bar. But I was glad I went. I ran into a very popular student friend from the Christian college that I had attended. His lover was a prominent ex-staff member. That evening I found out that several members of our fraternity were gay, as well as other friends, but we were all afraid to admit it to each other at the time because we thought we were sinful. We could have eliminated so much of our struggle and loneliness if we had only been honest, but our religious tradition would not allow it. Unknown to all of us, we had the makings of an underground gay student organization — with a faculty advisor, too. This drove home the fact that I was not the only gay Christian in the world. At that same bar I met ministers, a popular local gospel disc jockey and even a grammy award-winning gospel music star.

"There is something to be said for these gospel queens," a friend of mine once said sarcastically. "How many choirloft spaces, organ benches and pulpits would be empty if they all stayed home?"

It was a few months after this experience that I arrived in Philadelphia on a Sunday afternoon and was afraid to be seen buying a *Gay News*. I had fully accepted who I was and decided to work on being as happy as I possibly could, but there was still a lot to loose by becoming openly gay. I would surely jeopardize my job. At the age of twenty-four I was still living with my parents. They would probably become rude to my friends and begin to censor my telephone calls. My conservative friends would disown me. I had become a linguist and aspired to pursue my Latin American interests through an international organization such as the United Nations or the Organization of American States. Would I risk such an opportunity for the sake of becoming an openly gay man?

For three years I lived as a selectively invisible gay man leading a double life, but eventually I moved out of my parents' house. Then I reserved my invisibility only for family and work. Even after I told my mother, I was forced to remain closeted in the presence of family to avoid friction.

When I began to write for the gay press and subsequently went to work for the city's AIDS Control Program it suddenly occurred to me that my motives for being an invisible gay man had ceased to exist. Having moved into Center City to be close to work, I was living in a gay neighborhood, working in a situation where my sexual preference was often an asset and a known fact to my employers. Seeing my name in print for the first time in a gay publication felt very good. But sometimes I forgot that the rest of the world was not like this gay ghetto that I lived and worked in. Everyone was not free to be as visible as I was.

That message was driven home when I decided to stop working for the AIDS program and go to graduate school. Would I be a different person when I was uptown at school than when I was downtown at home? What if I became active in the gay student organization and the chairperson of my academic department found out? Would that motivate her to choose one of the other three equally qualified students for that one available graduate assistantship? Suppose I want to apply for a job there when I graduate?

Some individuals may choose to forego open acknowledgement of their sexual preference in order to fight another unpopular cause, such as my friend in Nicaragua. I know someone else who feels he must remain closeted because he is an elementary school teacher without tenure.

That might work well for them. They would probably argue that it is a matter of dire necessity and that it is well worth the sacrifice. Be that as it may, I can no longer deny who I am. I have no specific strategy for my future — I will cross each bridge when I come to it.

▼

Lawrence W. O'Connor

Chicago, Illinois

The End of a Long Silence

I was aware of my homosexuality at a very young age. As early as kindergarten, I found myself attracted to other boys. At a rollerskating rink in second grade, I wondered why two girls could skate together holding hands but not two boys. I never had trouble understanding or accepting myself, I only wondered how I would be able to live in a world filled with people who disliked the way I was.

While growing up, love was something I watched other people experience and enjoy. My brothers, cousins, and friends always had another person with whom to go places and do things; someone with whom to share everything. The countless men I secretly loved and fantasized about were only in private, empty dreams in which the love was never returned. I seemed to be the only person in the world with no need for love and companionship.

Adolescence was a very difficult period in my life. Instead of being a time of change and sexual maturity, it was a time for standing still. My straight friends "came out" naturally during adolescence. They learned to date and establish relationships. All I learned to do was hide what I was feeling.

Throughout high school and college I had no way to meet people of the same age and sexual orientation. These were more years of isolation and secrecy. I saw what other guys my age did, listened to what they said and how they felt. I was expected to be part of a world with which I had nothing in common.

During college I worked part-time in a factory outlet store which specialized in giftware and Christmas decorations. Many of their customers were gay. I came to know many of these people on a personal level, especially a guy named Cliff. I learned he was gay and lived with another man. As we developed a sense of trust, he realized that I had few social outlets and never mentioned a girlfriend. I was very knowledgeable about homosexuality, and he began to ask if I was gay. I denied the truth for months but finally exposed my deepest, darkest secret one day over lunch.

It was August 1984. I was twenty-four years old and had never told anyone. Having recently graduated from college, I was planning to leave my home in Chicago that fall to attend nursing school in a small town near Eau Claire, Wisconsin. I had planned to stay in my family's summer house in Eau Claire County, isolated from the world, and spend the rest of my life there.

I never intended to come out. I had always taken for granted that I would remain closeted, running from the truth. I found it inconceivable that I had rights and privileges just like straight people.

All through my life there had never been a role model to look up to or anyone to help me deal constructively with being gay: no family, no relatives, teachers, clergy, no peer support. The best libraries in the city had more books on breeding hamsters than on homosexuality. Evil, wicked people like Anita Bryant or Jerry Falwell were always in the background adding fear to the confusion. I was never exposed to anything positive about being gay, only to the myths and stereotypes spread by ignorant people.

However, I had told one person. It was the end of a long silence. Overnight my entire way of thinking changed: I realized that I had a life to live just the same as anyone else, and that my sexuality should be my birthright. I had to begin to be myself or go on forever being what somebody else wanted me to be.

I remained in Chicago that fall doing a lot of thinking and reading. In October, a talk show sex therapist, Phyllis Levy, read over the air a coming out letter I had written to her program. The following week, I called the telephone hotline at Gay Horizons, Chicago's gay and lesbian social service agency. I was very nervous and didn't know where to begin talking. After about two minutes, my parents came home and I was forced to hang up. I called the following night and was able to talk uninterrupted. It was an unfortunate situation to find in a total stranger the support and understanding my own family could never provide.

The following week, I joined a ten-week men's coming out group at Horizons. In the group were twelve guys my own age in similar situations. Each week we discussed a different aspect of being gay. In addition, a male nurse gave a lecture on AIDS and other sexually transmitted diseases. One week we heard from a male couple who had been together for ten years. Another week the group went on a field trip to a variety of gay bars. It was the first visit to a gay bar for some of the people in the group, including me.

In November, I talked with a parish priest concerning my homosexuality. He was somewhat receptive but advised that I should at least *try* dating women. As a gay Catholic, I began attending the Dignity masses about the middle of November. At Dignity, I joined another support group run by Fr. Bob, a Catholic priest ministering to the Dignity community. Through role playing in the group, I learned many valuable lessons about coming out to people that would be helpful later with my family.

Early in the coming out process, I had decided my parents must know eventually. I have always been a stranger living in their house. Living at home in hiding, I was very careful about using the phone, receiving mail and reading certain books. I lied about going out. It was hard to develop gay friendships because much of my personal life had to be kept a secret. One slip, one mistake, might mean the end of everything. I hadn't the faintest idea how my parents would react. The greatest fear I had was that I would be disowned by my family. I felt that was the worst tragedy I could face.

I began telling a few close family friends. I wrote to my Aunt Dee, a psychiatric social worker, and received her support. I came out to my brothers, who both responded positively. I found it amusing that during the two separate conversations with them, both said they now understand why I never played baseball and football with the other neighborhood boys when we were younger. Of all the straight people I talked with, my sister-in-law was the most supportive — she drew none of her own conclusions nor doubted my word; she didn't tell me I was confused, going through a phase, or that I hadn't met the right woman yet. Instead, she listened and tried to understand the best she could.

Finally, on the night of February 12th, 1985, I found the courage to tell my parents. The fear was so intense at first, it was hard to begin talking. I was actually shaking and gasping for air; it felt as if someone was standing on my stomach. As time went on, I became more relaxed, talked freely and answered a lot of questions.

My parents' reactions were totally different. My father had retired from the U.S. Postal Service. As a letter carrier, his routes were situated in the most heavily-concentrated gay areas of Chicago. He knew countless gays as businessmen, bar owners and neighborhood residents. I was surprised when he told me he had never known a more honest and ambitious, hard-working group of people. He said I must be prepared to face many obstacles in my lifetime as a homosexual but that I would face none from him.

My mother is a housewife who judged gay people solely on the basis of prejudice. Her exposure to homosexuality was limited to the drag queens and effeminate men the TV networks seem to highlight each year during the Gay Pride parade. The many stories concerning AIDS have also made her afraid. She was not willing to talk or listen, only saying I was disgraceful and must keep all aspects of my homosexuality out of her life completely.

Being different has not been easy in the unaccepting and oppressive atmosphere in which I grew up. Coming out has been even more painful — however, the lie I was living would never have stopped hurting. Life is too short to spend anymore time and energy being someone I'm not!

Coming out is proving to be the most productive and liberating experience of my life. The sense of freedom I am experiencing is overwhelming. I've met many new people and have become very involved in my community, without experiencing guilt or feeling threatened. I feel as though I've been reborn into a life with a whole new purpose and direction. And yet, I am the same person as always. The only difference is now I'm living freer and more openly, experiencing greater happiness, and being much more honest about myself.

After being out for two years, I have yet to have a boyfriend or be sexual with another person. This will come with time. I have had several chances for casual sex but I need something more for myself. It was too hard to grow up, come out and find a good job. I want to live and make up for time lost, not act carelessly and die of AIDS. I'm seeking a lasting, monogamous relationship. I'll have to be very lucky and he'll have to be very special.

Jim Baxter
Raleigh, North Carolina

First Class Mail

In the summer of 1974, as I looked forward to my twenty-first birthday, the idea of "coming of age" meant only one thing to me: "coming out." I wanted to be up-front and honest. "No more lies," I said to myself. "No more hiding. Ever."

As far back as I can remember, I have always known I was homosexual – although I certainly didn't know the word. The earliest sexual arousal I can specifically recollect was in response to a picture of bare-chested TV cowboy star Clint Walker. Later, from about the age of thirteen on, I was as sexually active as opportunity allowed. Those encounters (which lasted through high school) were mostly anonymous "quickies" but, even so, they were the best part of an otherwise unhappy adolescence.

At first I was too excited at being found sexually attractive to really consider the down side of my activities. I did eventually learn the word "homosexual," along with a good many others: "queer," "tearoom," "jailbait." I never felt particularly guilty about my sexuality (except perhaps for the sordid places in which I found partners). I did feel guilty about leading two separate lives, about having to lie and keep secrets.

When I enrolled at American University in Washington, D.C., it meant continuing to live at home in the Maryland suburbs. My relationship with my mother, who raised me by herself, was always difficult at best. By the time I got to college, we had only managed to reach a kind of guarded truce.

Among my complaints about A.U., and I had many, was the absence of any gay student group on campus. I eventually found an organization at the University of Maryland, where they had a gay "coffee house" on Friday nights. I made up my mind to go.

The group met in a sizable lounge in the cavernous Student Union building. After I finally found the room, I hesitated. There were perhaps thirty people inside, men and women, black and white, not all of them strictly college age. What if they didn't like me? What if I didn't like them? I paced back and forth outside the door for an eternity, then suddenly bolted at top speed into and across the room.

I skidded to a halt next to the refreshment table, stood stiff as a board and wondered what on earth I was going to do next. Fortunately, a kind man came over to me and said "hello." After that, the rest was easy.

Out of those Friday night gatherings came a lot of experience: several short but intense love affairs; other, more activist meetings; the discovery of gay newspapers and books. All my involvement, however, came to an end when I transferred to Guilford College, a small Quaker school in Greensboro, North Carolina.

In many respects, I was happier at Guilford than I'd ever been in my life: I was enthusiastic about my studies, made lots of new friends, got *involved.* But I was back in the closet. I was at a loss to find the kind of community I'd experienced in D.C.; "gay liberation" had not as yet reached the South.

Once I moved away from home, I seldom went back. Living in Greensboro was cheap, so I stayed and worked during the summers. When I did go back for a visit, I spent most of my time with gay people at group meetings and dances; it was years before I ever went to a gay bar. Living in North Carolina was good for me, mostly: I learned how to make my own way in the world, gained a lot of self-confidence. But I still longed for a gay community like the one I had known.

Finally, in June of 1974, I thought I saw a chance to put the experiences I'd had in D.C. to good use. There was a small, independent paper publishing locally then, called *The Greensboro Sun*. An editorial mentioned the need for "new blood and ideas." So I offered myself and suggested an article, or a series of articles, about gay liberation.

The editor, Rev. Jim Clark, who also headed something called the "Inter-Church Ministry for Social Change," wrote back to me just a few days later:

> I would be very interested in your writing a column for us on an experimental basis. I like your educational approach, for this fits in with our desire to provide the facts for public discussion of the issue.
>
> A little advice: since we are trying to build a broad readership, it is best to tend away from language which might be considered "obscene." While my own feeling is that such words as "war" and "nigger" are obscene, many of those we are trying to reach are easily turned off by any language other than what they thought Nixon used to talk.

I titled my column "On Being Gay," and the first installment ran in the July issue:

> A friend once commented that there was no greater anxiety among us than that of homosexuality. The best solution to this, I felt and he didn't, was open discussion and education. I am now in the process of such an education. I am coming out, and I am learning a great deal.
>
> My friends, wonderfully, have not rejected me, nor do they seem to feel sad for me because, I think, they can see I am happy with being gay...
>
> This unexpected attitude among my friends reflects, I'm sure, the efforts of those who have

> struggled for sexual freedom these past twenty years, bringing this issue to the media, long before I decided to take advantage of their struggle. Now I wish to join them.
>
> This space, then, is not simply for my declaration: it is to reach you, the gay people of Greensboro. For in discovering myself, I have also discovered some things about us: that we are not bad, but rather possess a rare and valuable quality; that we are not alone, for twenty million make quite a crowd even in America; that we are not powerless, and many across the country are fighting for their rights. . .

Rev. Clark ran the column with some trepidation and waited to see what sort of reaction it would provoke. Happily, my next column was preceded by the following editor's note:

> Last issue we began running this column as an experiment, requesting reader response. Jim Baxter received more mail than any columnist in the history of *The Sun*. Thanks.

This historic flood of mail amounted to exactly seven letters — four of them from gay friends I'd coerced into writing. And it included one incredibly confused response, which at the time I thought was too funny to be angry about:

> Dear Gay Columnist:
>
> We do understand your dilemma. You are right in wanting open discussion and education on this matter. If I were giving advice to all gays — I would first ask if you have considered seeing your family physician? He will keep this matter confidential. He may know of someone that could be of more help to you. It could be possible that minor surgery would erase your problem. I am sure you are aware of the fact that surgery is now possible that will change a person from one sex to another if that person was born with a defect. If you have a minister by all means see him.

We are all put here on earth for a purpose. Seek and find out what your purpose is in life. I don't know if you believe in God, but if you do you will know God put men on the earth to help multiply and women as his helpmate. If all men were Gays, the earth would cease to exist for man, as there would be no men or women left to populate the world. The Bible has all the answers on this subject, so please try reading it.

Sincerely,
Bea

Little did I realize that more than a decade later there would still be an appalling number of people writing letters very much like that one.

When I wrote, in that first column, that "my friends, wonderfully, have not rejected me," I was exaggerating. I had only told a couple of people, and the process had been tedious. Was I going to have to go through this with everyone, I wondered. Would I always have to phrase the statement ever so carefully, worried that it might be interpreted as a heart-rending confession or an admission of some guilty secret? Would I always have to listen to an equally careful response, one that told me nothing of how my friend really felt?

There had to be a quicker, easier way to get this "coming out" business over with! That, I think, was at least part of my motivation to write a newspaper column. For one thing, it was more efficient. I wanted to reach the greatest number of people with the least amount of effort. For another, it was easier to summon the necessary courage. The circumstance of coming out in print made it very easy to avoid direct confrontation, to avoid risking rejection.

My essay for the September issue — the first one all my friends at school would see — was written while I was visiting home in August. While I was there, I also had what was, perhaps the most intense one-night stand of my life. It began with dinner and ended — almost twenty-four hours later — with a long, passionate kiss, out in public, on a sidewalk just off Dupont Circle. Back at my mother's apartment, full of passionate fervor, I sat down at the typewriter and pounded out my declaration to Greensboro and North Carolina:

> The fact remains that gays here are not free. Being gay means being free to love all people, of either sex — but until we change the conditioning under which we live, we are free only to *try* to love, against great odds. *There is a new gay world, it is real, it is growing, and it is worth fighting for.* It is a world that offers alternatives, that recognizes that gay means more than the sterile, showy glitter and camp we now associate with the word. Can't you see it? Gay people are no longer servile, harmless and invisible members of the community, but part of the world as a whole. It *can* happen here. Isn't it worth the risks involved?

The day that issue rolled off the presses, I left dozens of copies lying all over campus, many of them open to my page. And in some cases, slid it under the door of certain individuals' rooms.

For the next couple of weeks I got responses ranging from "You're not *that* Jim Baxter, are you?" to "There *are* two Jim Baxters, aren't there?" After that, people got used to the idea.

I had wanted to be honest with my friends about my sexuality, and had managed to do that. But, even though the September issue of *The Sun* was out all over campus, there was still the matter of telling my mom.

I had long suspected that she had a secret of her own to tell me, just as I had one to tell her. When I was home in August, I said, as I was leaving to come back to Greensboro, "I want you to write me a letter on my twenty-first birthday next month, and I want you to tell me the truth." In honor of my most significant birthday, I thought, my mother and I would be open and honest with each other.

And so we were. She told me I was illegitimate. I told her I was homosexual. It was something of an impasse: neither of us was in a position to call the other names. Her letter to me began:

> Dear Jim:
>
> You surprised me with your request for a

"Birthday" letter as I expected to tell you. I'm not sure exactly what you want to know but will try to tell you anyhow.

To begin with, your father and I never quite got married. We were supposed to be "engaged" and made some plans, but I guess he really didn't want to be tied down.

When I found I was pregnant, I really didn't know what to do. I visited certain well-known agencies but didn't get much help so made up my own mind to keep the baby. However, I didn't quite know how to handle it afterwards. As a government employee, my record would follow me from job to job — so I couldn't pretend to be married. Also, in those McCarthy times, everyone was investigated for "suitability." The only way I could figure to do was to lead a double life. . .

A few days later, I wrote back:

Dear Mom:

Your letter casts a whole different light on a lot of years! I'm very proud of you — really — for both the courage you showed in writing that letter and the courage you've shown in living with me these past twenty-one years. And I thank you — I'm glad you decided to raise me. It took a lot of guts and I realize now how awfully rough it must have been. The news had several effects on me — all of them rather profound but none of them bad. There are a lot of things I'd like to say — how I'd like to apologize for a lot of misjudgements, and how I understand and respect you for keeping the facts to yourself, but mostly I'd like to say thank you. Damn — I've got all kinds of respect for you.

So, turnabout being fair play and all that: if you're going to tell me your big secret, I should be ready to tell you mine. Well, you did and I am, although you may have already put things together for yourself (I wouldn't be surprised!). The news,

> briefly, is this: as I come to settle down in the next couple of years, I may as likely settle down with a man as with a woman. This is no recent development — homosexual relationships have been a part of my life for a long, long time . . . None of this is anybody's fault (if you go looking for blame) — you certainly didn't "fail" me in any respect and I hope you don't feel that I've failed you. There are many positive aspects to the world in which "those people" (of which I am one) live — some are already present and some are there if you work for them.
>
> I am enclosing copies of a column I write for a community newspaper here. It's a recent development and part of my efforts to live in one world and not several — separated by lies and evasions. All of my friends down here know my story and they still feel the same way about me — they even threw a smashing birthday party for me which I'll tell you about some other time.
>
> So, there 'tis. I hope, as I said, that you take the news well. I feel better for the honesty. Don't you?
>
> Love,
> Jim

A few days passed, and then I got a letter back from Mom:

> I was glad to get your letter, as I guess I was waiting for a reaction! You make me sound nobler than I am as it was probably an essentially selfish action. I guess the hardest part was having to "live a lie" as I don't lie very well and don't like to lie at all. It is much better to have things out in the open, with everyone.
>
> I can't really say your news was a total surprise. I seem to "know" a lot of things on a psychic level without conscious thought.
>
> My feelings are somewhat mixed on this, as on many subjects, partly because I was brought up

in an era when there were no alternatives. I'm sure you know that I am a strong believer in individual rights and freedom. At the same time, I don't really like Gay organizations any more than I like Black militant organizations or Jewish organizations. Although I realize it is necessary to organize to achieve change and fight discrimination, I feel that "exclusiveness" is in the long run stultifying and the individual needs to constantly broaden his horizons.

I also feel that sex — of any kind — is a private thing between two consenting individuals and dislike public displays but then again that may be my upbringing.

I admire your stand, and your effort to find your way. I hope that you can resolve your own conflicts in the ways that are best for you.

As a comment: and not looking to change you, but the "Dear Gay" letter reminded me that I have often thought you might have a hormonal imbalance relating to my own and the shots I took — so if you think such a problem might be a factor a medical check might be in order.

Thanks for telling me — I really appreciate the fact that you have over the years told me many of your feelings and problems as so many people can't talk to their parents at all.

Keep fighting for what you believe in!

Love,

Mom

P.S. As somebody once told me, the truth won't change your real friends and the others don't matter — and it's true!

Before I could respond to that remark about "hormones," she sent me another letter with a few additional questions:

Upon further consideration of your letter, I am still

> a bit confused. Perhaps if you were willing to answer some questions for me, I would better understand your position.
>
> Are any of your friends that I know gay, or do you have other "circles?" As a college student, have you actually experienced discrimination, etc.? I shouldn't think it would be a significant factor in campus life, particularly if you don't have the effeminate characteristics that people react to. What are the "good points" you spoke of, besides being honest?
>
> Very possibly my questions derive mostly from my own appalling ignorance due to naivete, lack of contact or exposure and in general, ignorance. As you can imagine, my psychology background only exposed me to the kind of psychiatric junk that we all deplore and which tends to speak in stereotypes.
>
> Anyhow, if you wouldn't mind telling me more about your thoughts and feelings, I would be a better-informed person. Above all, I hope that whatever you choose will result in close and lasting human relationships, which is the most important thing.
>
> Love,
> Mom

By the end of September, my "coming out" was all over. The newspaper column continued for another year. My mom and I began talking to one another as adults, on equal footing, and we both made an effort to put the unhappy past behind us.

There is an epilogue to this story, one that took place just recently. Thirteen years later, I work as editor and publisher of a local gay newspaper. My mother, who retired from her government job, settled in North Carolina.

A rare family reunion was being planned this past spring, and my mother made a strong appeal for me to be there. I'm not very close to my relatives, and I had mixed feelings about spending time with a bunch of people who still called me "Jimmy," and remembered me mostly as a pudgy little cherub.

I also had questions about going through this "coming out" business again. Sitting down with her at her kitchen table, I said, "Mom, this reunion means a lot to you. I'd like to know how you'd like me to behave. I'm not saying that I'll do what you ask, but I'd like to know how you feel." She looked puzzled. "How do I respond when they start asking me why I'm not married?"

After an uncomfortable minute of silence, she said, "Well, you don't have to answer. I mean, you could just brush the question off."

I wasn't pleased with that answer, but I thought I'd just let it go. I was still undecided about whether or not to go, when I got a phone call from Mom about two days later.

"Look," she said, "I've been thinking about what we were talking about the other day. I just wanted to tell you that I think you should do whatever you think is right. You tell them exactly what you want to."

That was exactly the answer I'd been hoping for.

Scot Roskelley

Portland, Oregon

Coming Out to My Wife

It was one of those sultry summer evenings — the kind you long for in the middle of a January ice storm — the kind Portland is so famous for. After finishing dinner, our five-year-old son scurried outside to join the neighbors' kids, leaving his mother and me at the dinner table.

My wife Julie had begun seeing a counselor five months earlier and was dealing with a bad case of "identity crisis." She was changing dramatically — turning into a person of her own making rather than a mirror image of her parents or husband. And as she changed, so did our relationship. I was at a loss as to how to relate to this new person; this person who for all her change seemed to still be suffering emotional agony.

Observing all of this caused my own introspection. Who was I? What did I really want out of a relationship? And was I getting it, or would I ever get it?

Over the months while Julie searched for her new identity, I built a protective wall around myself. As she tried to penetrate my secure fortress, she became even more frustrated. Communication had reached a standstill over the weeks, and here we were at the dinner table.

"What is going to become of us?" I asked, fearful of the consequences of this conversation. This was the first time I had ever cast doubt on our future together.

Julie proceeded to describe the defenses she perceived I was building, concluding with the recommendation that I, too, seek counseling. Having watched what Julie had gone through, I was well aware that psychologists probe into every recess of your inner being. If I were to deal with my tangled emotions, it would mean bringing everything out in the open.

"Julie," I said, "the things I might have to deal with as a result of counseling will no doubt involve you and are things you shouldn't have to deal with until you've finished counseling and are in a better emotional state."

Worried that the proverbial cat was on its way out of the bag, I began clearing dishes from the table as a diversion.

It didn't work.

All the while, Julie pursued this same vein. "If there are things you're going to bring out, I don't see why we can't work on them now. What could they be? What are you talking about?" she asked.

Five minutes of a cat-and-mouse game ensued. I was washing the dishes, and Julie was drying.

"Scot?" she asked while drying a drinking glass, "Are you gay?"

The question brought on a sudden wave of nausea. And I immediately realized that my response could dramatically change the course of my life in the next hour, the next month, and even the next year. The effects would be longstanding. And they meant change.

I was tired of change. I had been riding an emotional roller coaster for four months now watching *her* change. I was looking for an end to change, not a beginning.

Yet, years before, I had resolved that *if she were to ask,* I must give the honest answer.

Panic squeezed every muscle. The few seconds spent rationalizing my decision seemed like hours. And I became acutely aware that to hesitate much longer was to affirm her suspicion.

"Let's finish the dishes first and then sit down and talk," I answered. The following ten minutes in the kitchen were, and no doubt will always be, the longest ten minutes of my life.

With the kitchen clean, we sat on the couch and I poured out my story. I had felt attracted to men as long as I could remember, but to act upon that feeling was impossible in my mind. My religious upbringing had taught me that God frowned on homosexual activity. And besides, as a youth, I lived in a rednecked town tucked away in the California Sierras. Homosexuality was akin to things like murder and incest in the eyes of the community. I was quite certain I was the *only* one in the entire county of 22,000 people to feel the way I felt.

I attended a church-operated liberal arts college in the mid-seventies, which helped reinforce the "sin concept" of homosexuality. Fulfilling the expectations of society, I dated women throughout my college years, assuming that my desire for men would subside.

One day, I met a woman who lit "something" within me. It was instant enchantment. Julie had the same zest for life that I had. And we enjoyed so many of the same things. As time rolled by, I came to the conclusion that there would never be anyone whose company I could enjoy more than hers.

And, miracle of miracles, she even awakened a spark of sexual desire in me. At last, these homosexual feelings would be put to rest.

In 1977 we were married and moved to Los Angeles.

Time passed, and those feelings didn't disappear. Instead, they grew stronger. In October of 1979, while my wife was six months pregnant with our son, I realized these feelings were here to stay. I knew I had control over how I responded, but I had not control over the feelings themselves. It was then that I finally accepted that I was gay.

On the heels of this realization, I had my first gay sexual experience. Afterward, I never again doubted my true sexual orientation.

I became active in a local organization of professional gay men. For the first time, I saw gay men who were just like me. They were teachers, doctors, priests, and architects. Where were the sex-crazed perverts society had warned me about? These were decent, respectable, hard-working people. Seeing them helped me accept myself in a way nothing else could.

What was most difficult to accept was how I could reconcile my homosexuality with my marriage. I loved my wife. I thought she was a great person and couldn't ever conceive of finding anyone, male or female, that I could be more compatible with. The only problem with her was the packaging. And that was a significant problem.

Months wore on. There were more sexual encounters. And then, I was transferred to the Pacific Northwest. Absorbed in the tedium of a new job, acquiring new friends, and raising a son, the sexual encounters came to a halt. But the acceptance of my sexuality remained the same. So did the attraction to men.

Several years later, Julie and I became acquainted with a man named David. I'd met him through my business contacts as a public relations director. I had strong suspicions that he was gay, and after several months and a visit to his apartment, I was certain of it. A quote on his refrigerator, "They condemn that which they do not understand," was all I needed to see.

Weeks later, I confessed my own homosexuality to him and my hunch about David was confirmed. Over time, we became close friends, strictly platonic, and drew Julie into our friendship. It was like one of those tight threesomes you see in the movies. We did everything together, went everywhere together . . . to the point that it might have appeared odd to outsiders.

We shared *so* much.

But there was one secret we both kept camouflaged from Julie — our sexuality. And while she couldn't put her finger on it, *she knew* there was something about this relationship she wasn't sharing equally. There were times when she felt like an outsider among us — like when we were served by a good-looking waiter or every time Mark Harmon appeared in a beer commercial.

Eventually, we felt it was necessary for David to divulge his sexuality. And Julie, who had never before had any close association with a gay person, went through the typical processing of this revelation. First came the questions: "How long have you felt this way?" "Did you choose to be this way?" "Are you sure about this?"

Then came the uneasiness. David was a person she liked a lot

. . . even loved. Yet, he was something she had always decided she didn't approve of. Either her opinion of David had to change, or her opinion of homosexuality had to change.

David and I watched her assimilate the messages. We studied her reactions over the next few days and weeks. We knew this might be a precursor to my eventual coming out to Julie.

In time, she became comfortable with David's homosexuality. She read more on the subject. She watched talk shows on TV. And she became an ardent defender of the gay cause.

This change in her views on homosexuality triggered a rethinking of many of her longstanding values and was the catalyst for her beginning counseling. Over a period of six months, she changed considerably. The person I once knew no longer existed. Yet, the new person was still not fully developed. The "old Julie" and the "new Julie" were at war with each other. The transition period was long, and the effect on our relationship was immense.

To say that she took the news that I was gay with "the bat of an eye" would be a lie. However, the road had been paved with David. She knew that she could love a significant other who was gay. She knew she wasn't "less of a woman" because I was gay. Now, she was faced with whether she could love a husband, a sexual partner, who was gay, and continue a contractual relationship with that person.

Interestingly, my coming out to Julie improved our communication and served as a vehicle to tear down barriers we had built over the preceding months.

This was a crucial turning point in my life. I was at a fork in the road where I could say, "I love you, but I want out of the marriage so I can pursue a more ideal relationship with someone of my own sex."

Or I could say, "I love you and will repress sexual feelings, remaining faithful to you forever."

Or I could say, "I love you and want to make the marriage work, but I also want my sexual freedom."

I loved Julie. About that, there was no doubt. We had made it through bad times and good times. We shared many similar interests. And until recently, we had always communicated openly and resolved conflict well. I couldn't conceive of finding anyone I could be more compatible with. Thoughts ran through my mind of searching for the perfect man the rest of my life and ending up lonely because I never found him.

We discussed the future over and over again. The outcome was that we both loved each other. Julie felt she couldn't compel me to cloister my sexuality, and I didn't want to. We decided to pursue our relationship, taking it one day at a time. Neither of us knew of any other married couples that had remained together once one of them had announced his or her homosexuality. Yet, we were willing to forge what to us appeared to be a new trail.

We sought as much information and input as possible, talking with a gay priest, a gay counselor, and members of the local chapter of Parents and Friends of Lesbians and Gays. We discovered a professional couple with children, where the man is gay, that has remained happily married for over twenty years. We also discovered a family with a husband, a wife, and the wife's lesbian lover and her three children. While many in the gay community are skeptical about the success of a relationship such as Julie's and mine, they have been extremely supportive of our giving it a try. The love and concern shown for us has been overwhelming.

I am currently involved with another married man who has two children. Ours is a fairly new relationship. My wife is aware of this man's presence in my life, but does not want details. His wife is aware of his sexual orientation, but not of his current involvement with another man. Juggling two relationships is *not* easy. and it may not work forever. I could fall deeply in love with this man and feel the need to leave. She could decide she has compromised herself by remaining with a gay husband and leave.

Neither Julie nor I know what the future holds. Nonetheless, we are committed to our love for each other. Life is a process, and whether or not a marriage contract binds us together in the coming years, that love and concern for each other will always remain.

▼

Vernon Maulsby

Graterford, Pennsylvania

Nightwings

I grew up in the sixties, between Acid Rock and Rock and Roll. Just before I entered my teens I had my first crush and lover. His name was Eddie; a slim, dark-eyed boy, perhaps a year younger than I was. We had always been inseparable as children; we seemed a natural team, and our families gave no notice. No one thought it odd that we preferred each other's company over other people's. We were known and accepted as loners, plus neither one of us was popular in or out of school . . . me 'cause of my obesity and color, Eddie 'cause of his habitually long silences when all he wanted to do was think about things or write his poetry.

In 1969 we became lovers. It wasn't planned or expected — it just happened one day while we were stretched out together on the couch watching TV. His parents had just told him about their upcoming divorce and custody fight. Neither parent wanted him and made it evident. He cried in my arms; I felt angry and wanted to protect him, shield him from the pain. I had butterflies in my stomach and felt feverish. He looked up while I held him and kissed me. We slowly, fumblingly made love, and I felt complete for the first time in my life. Nothing ever felt so right before. We cleaned up in the shower and went back to watching TV.

We never made love again. What came naturally to me was "wrong" to Eddie. Our friendship was soon on the skids, and we consciously avoided each other. The word "homosexual," or the thought of being gay, never entered my mind. I was just me, and I thought Eddie was a once-in-a-lifetime love.

Sex, of any kind, was a forbidden subject in my home. All I ever remember hearing was that when the "right" person came along I would know it. I know they meant a woman, but to my family that was an obvious fact that didn't need mentioning. In my highly religious home, lots of things were taken for granted with no effort made to spell them out. As a member of the only black family in an upper middle class suburb in upstate New York, there was a certain distance between me and normal social interaction. Being the minister's grandson, and fat too, I was really on my own, even as far as my moral precepts went. Eddie felt right, and that was enough.

In my early teens I had my first experience with females. I was capable physically, but something was missing. I thought that was just how straight sex was supposed to be, so I accepted my lack of enthusiasm as normal.

I was always one of those kids who wandered around town, just killing time — especially after Eddie and I broke up. One evening I was sitting on the pier, watching the Hudson River go by, when I met my first gay person. He was a cute guy in his thirties, just wandering around like me. We spoke for awhile, and I started feeling butterflies, like before. We stopped talking and just looked at each other. I was scared and happy at the same time as I took him home. My mom was out, so it was safe, and I wanted this man in my bed so bad my teeth itched. Later I learned his name was Terri; he was the guy that they had talked about in town as being "queer." I began to panic. What if someone had seen us together? He understood and left his phone number in case I wanted to meet him again.

We snuck around together for a couple of years. He cared enough about me to put up with my crap without complaints. He just lived as an example of how it could be and was patient with me. In 1973, he told me he was in love with me and wanted me to either move in, or at least admit that I was gay and stop hiding.

So, as far as my social life went, I came out. Terri helped me find my space. His advice was always available. He let me try my wings and was always there when I landed hard. He understood about my continued hiding from my parents and didn't press me — he said it would come with time and that I'd know when I was ready.

Until he moved in 1975, we were a couple. I didn't go with him, because as I had grown I learned that my needs had changed. We remained close friends until his death in 1982.

I went through a rough time about his death; he died by his own hand. We had spoken by phone the week before it happened, and, as far as I could tell, he was okay. He just came home from work and cut his wrists in the bathtub.

The services were closed to me once the family heard my name, but I made it to the graveside and paid my respects. I managed to put my bracelet in the grave so something of me could be with him. That may sound silly, but it felt right.

After I graduated from high school, I moved into my own apartment and began college. I worked in a hospital, and there I met my lover Percy. When I first saw him it was no big thing, but in the next few days I stopped in to check on his recovery. I knew he was gay the second time I talked to him, but things didn't gel until, as I was leaving one day, he threw his shorts at my head and walked naked into his bathroom. I'm lucky he had a private room, because we didn't wait. When he got released I left work early to take him home.

When Percy and I made plans to live together, I knew it was time to be honest with my mom. I made a big thing of it, rehearsing for weeks in front of my mirror while shaving, in the car on the way to school, and so on. I made reservations at this nice restaurant for us; I wanted everything just right.

Things went completely wrong. I ended up telling her over tea that afternoon. I just looked into her eyes and told her. My prepared speech (with historical footnotes) went right out the window. As I talked with my mother and told her I was gay and had been as long as I could remember, she just sat there sipping her tea. She took her glasses off, smiled, and told me she had known for years. After my jaw closed I started to cry; I couldn't help it. The pressure was off, and I couldn't stop. She held me tight, and we had a good cry together. I didn't lose her love as I had feared: she didn't like my choice, but she supported me. We became closer as the years passed.

The rest of the family ostracized me. I was no longer welcome in their homes or around their children. They feared that my gayness was contagious. My cousins were told that I was "sick" and they should stay away from me. It hurt, but Mom and Percy helped me get through it. Since my mother's death in 1982, my family and I live our own lives. Our contacts are few and far between.

My growth as a black gay person has been gradual, nurtured by both straight and gay people who loved me for who I am. Today I am free to live and love as I choose because of their support.

I have my wings
and Now
I can Fly.

Laurence Wolf

Cincinnati, Ohio

Is It Ever Too Late?

V*e get too soon oldt undt too late schmart.*

I have no reason to doubt that old Pennsylvania Dutch saying, and I've doubted plenty of things in my day. Today, I'm learning that a man *can* love me. All the reward I need from him is the smile on his face, the joy in his eyes, and the sincerity in his voice as he tells me that he is happy I've come into his life. Just in the nick of time, you might say: we recently celebrated his seventieth and my sixty-fifth birthdays.

When did I first know I was different? I was a "lefty" among right-handers in grade school. I was almost the only bookworm in the crowd. I was ill more often than the other children, and I gave a lot of thought to avoiding the neighborhood bullies. I was different. So, when the rest of the guys suddenly became interested in girls and I didn't, it was like everything else in my life . . . they went one way and I went another.

My first same-sex experience was in junior high. Herbie liked me to stroke his penis, so we'd sneak up to the roof and make sure no one else was there. It was flat, with chimney stacks and stairway kiosks to hide behind. He never returned the favor, which annoyed me. Then Herbie moved away and there were no other Herbies, though I looked sharply for any sign of this "difference" among my small group of pals. No "older man" came along, either.

My energy went into a helluva lot of reading . . . novels, history, biography, and later on, politics. No one ever told me I was a faggot, so I just buried my sexuality deep inside. Any mention of sex was Absolutely Forbidden in our household, and my parents never showed any physical affection for each other. By the time I was in my teens they were arguing constantly, and although sexual topics entered into that, they used figures of speech to disguise them. By the time I'd taken a college course in psychology, I decided that I was a case of arrested development as far as sex was concerned. It was a popular theory at the time, and seemed to be a handy explanation.

My college years ended early because I was drafted to fight in the army during World War II. On a troop train one night the guy sharing my bunk fucked me. That was a nice new experience. I didn't say a word – sex was, after all, unspeakable – and he never brought it up again. After basic training, overnight passes became available. I found a bar full of men interested in other men, but I rarely went there because of my fear that someone from my battallion might show up. I had all I could handle just surviving the emotional strain of army wartime regimentation.

I eventually went overseas just in time for the end of the war in the Pacific, narrowly missing combat duty. During that time, my life resumed its usual sexlessness.

It took me a long time to recall what I had actually done those few nights when I had bunked with another guy in town. I finally remembered, dimly: I was the bottom. How did the other guy know what I wanted? How did we meet at the bar? Those memories are still repressed. At any rate, it was while I was in the army that I decided I should try to pursue the opposite sex.

When I tried to figure out what sort of woman I wanted, I came up with a list of characteristics that were utterly unrealistic. I had already lived so much of my life alone, I just reconciled myself to living the rest of it alone too. I buried myself in my work.

After the war I went to graduate school. My roommate introduced me to a blonde, petite, attractive young woman. We fell in love, married, and went off to my first professional employment together. My Terrible Problem was finally solved! Children came along, and with them a house in the suburbs, and then a finer house in town. When our youngest was in high school, my wife said she'd had enough of a husband who spent entirely too much time at his books. The divorce was amicable.

I owe my coming out to my closest friend. I'd known Bob for decades, as a friend and professional colleague. I had never had the slightest clue that he was gay. Then one day he dropped by my house and started to tell me that he was a queer, that psychiatric counseling had been no help, that he could no longer tolerate his internal conflicts, and that his wife and some of his children could not accept his gayness. I found myself interrupting him. I admitted, in almost a whisper, that I too was "sexually ambiguous."

When he left, I was in a daze. Honesty with my closest pal had made me voice, for the first time in my life, my most deeply hidden secret. From then on, I had not just a friend and colleague, but an elder brother. With his encouragement I went to the local gay bars with him and his lover. And although it was several years before I could go alone, I found I could dance there. I could never dance with a woman; there was always too much uncontrollable tension. Bob got me to join several gay organizations and, since functioning on committees comes naturally to me, this was a good way to become active in the gay scene.

After I came out, all the usual stereotypes I had about gay men crashed, one after another. I found I was walking with a quicker step and felt twenty years younger. I was euphoric whenever I entered a gay environment or felt the electric thrill of dancing in the midst of a mob of moving men. Euphoria was knowing in my heart that being gay was all right.

Frustration soon replaced euphoria, however — frustration at wanting someone to share my life with, someone with whom I could have intimate rapport, someone with whom to consummate my liberation, and not finding him. Everyone seemed to be looking for someone younger, giving me that "Oh-I-can't-see-you-because-you're-over-thirty" look. I thought that gay guys of my vintage were snugly in their closets where I'd never find them.

There was rage, too, surfacing as the years of frustration went by: rage at a society that preached equality and practiced bigotry, and rage at a gay community that segregated itself. I got a constriction in my gut when I read ads that specified "No fems!" or that meant someone less than half my age when an "older man" was sought. I found that most gay men were much too conservative for me. Where was the flamboyance, the defiant alienation, the individuality and creativity that gays were supposed to have?

It was about six years after my coming out that I met Jerry, my lover; six sexless years of new-found inner strength, of seeing the world in new ways, and of disillusionment and heartache. Bob had written a letter that was published in a local gay paper, to which Jerry replied. Knowing my painful loneliness, Bob passed Jerry's name and address to me, and a lively correspondence developed. We were both busy people, and it was several months before we met, but we began to "click" right away. I found acceptance, affection, intimacy, and the same wacky sense of humor that I have. I have found that my love muscle can be delightfully hard for longer than I ever thought possible; that the whole body is sensually sensational.

If only I'd known this fifty years ago!

Steve Nohava

Norfolk, Virginia

My Discovery of Me

My name is Steve Nohava. I was born on February 4, 1970. Until I was eleven, most of my life had been spent running around the U.S. with an alcoholic mother and a father who kept abandoning us. I lost five years of school, but I managed to learn about the world by reading brochures, books, and newspapers. I usually bore the brunt of my mother's behavior when she got drunk, since I was always around and my dad wasn't. We would argue, she'd throw beer bottles at me, hit me with a garden hoe, and often abandon me.

By June of 1981 I had been through thirty-one states. I began to wonder how I could ever make anything of myself if I continued to miss school and subject myself to my parents' continued abuse and neglect. Slowly but surely, I started wanting to get away from that life, and I began to think of ways to do so.

My chance came on a sunny day in late July. My mother and I were in downtown Norfolk at a city bus shelter. We were waiting for a bus when she suddenly gave me five dollars and said, "Take this and go see if there are any movies here. If not, come back."

I looked for fifteen minutes or so all over the downtown area, but I didn't find a single movie theater. When I got back to the bus stop, my mother was not there.

I immediately said to myself, "I am sick and tired of being neglected, abused, and abandoned just so my mother can continue to drink. I desperately need to try a different life. I give my mother exactly one hour to show up. If she doesn't, I will walk to that pay phone across the street, dial 911, and turn myself in to the police."

The hour slowly went by with no word from my mother. I walked to the phone, dialed 911, and when the man said "Norfolk Police," I said:

"My name is Steve Nohava. My mother abandoned me at the Granby Mall bus stop. She has done this to me several times before. I want to turn myself in to the police and start a new life."

Within minutes a cop car showed up and I went with them. I told them all that had happened in my life. I was told that I would be put in the custody of social services. I was in a shelter home until the courts put me in the custody of Chesapeake Social Services in August.

While I was in the shelter I had my first gay experience. Mark and I were roommates throughout my stay there. One day, while we were taking a nap, Mark climbed up to the top bunk and laid beside me. I didn't pay any mind. Then he moved his hand to my crotch and massaged me. He asked, "Do you mind?"

I replied, "No, it's okay." It felt so good, I began to get a hard-on. We massaged each other, and sucked each other off. We were both thoroughly pleased with this contact, and I asked Mark if we could do it again.

He replied, "Yes, whenever you want."

So we continued our "sessions of contact," as we called them, every night and every day at nap time. It was a sad moment when it came time to hug goodbye. We left the shelter on the same day; me to a foster home, Mark to his real home. We didn't have time to get each other's address. I will always remember him, for he helped me have the best moments of my life.

I began to notice I was different soon after I was put into foster and group homes in October of 1981. I saw people call each other "fairy," "homo," "fag," and "queer" simply because they were patting each other on the shoulder. I saw this in other teenagers and even some adults. I knew nothing about these words, but since I didn't do any name calling, I got teased, too.

I found that the only way to be safe from the harassment was to start showing interest in the opposite sex and have a girlfriend. I rejected that idea immediately, since I did not see what was so special about females. I had enjoyed my encounters with Mark.

The pressure of feeling and acting different began to mount. I looked up "homo," "faggot," and the other words in the dictionary and encyclopedia. Some I couldn't find; others were defined as "slang for homosexual." I turned to "homosexual" and "homosexuality." The definition read "a person attracted to members of the same sex or gender."

I couldn't believe that my peers and some adults put down homosexuals just because they exist. I had never rejected the idea of men enjoying the contact I had. I heard the news talk dirty about gays. Others mentioned how disgusting "it" was. Gays were often the objects of jokes. Even the church talked about how much of a sin gayness was. I could not find any books that didn't talk about homosexuality as a disease or a psychiatric disorder that should be treated. I felt that I was caught between my perfectly normal feelings and a homophobic society.

During the two years I was gathering this information, I felt there was no one to turn to. Once I saw this society for what it was, I could do nothing but cry because I feared I had to face ridicule, rejection, and loneliness because I performed sexual acts with men. I tried soul searching and prayer for a "cure." But I still had my deep desires for other guys.

In November of 1984 things began to turn around for me when I moved to a group home in northern Virginia. I had a counselor there who seemed open-minded and comforting. She noticed I was down in the dumps one day and asked what was wrong. I replied, "I'm not sure how you will take this, but I think you are open-minded enough to hear it. I think I might very well be a homosexual."

She said, "Okay. To me it wouldn't matter if the whole world was gay, but right now only ten percent of us are. Tell me, how did you come to this conclusion?"

I was totally shocked! Never before had I seen anyone react

so calmly and reassuringly to what I thought was a crisis. I went ahead and took up over an hour telling her my life story.

She told me that she found my life very interesting because she had had similar problems. Finally she said, "I have to go to a meeting now, but here are a couple of books I think will help you." She reached into her briefcase and pulled out two books: one entitled *One Teenager In Ten* and another called *Gays Among Us*.

I began to read them immediately. I felt reassured after reading the stories and knowing that the people who wrote them went through the same problems I did, and they found ways to press on in life. I no longer felt lonely. And I began to gain more wisdom and courage.

My counselor gave me permission to use the order form in the back of *One Teenager In Ten* to order more books. I immediately ordered *Young, Gay and Proud!* and several others. I read them as soon as they arrived. I was pleased and amazed to find information that I had not seen before, like "Gays have been around since Ancient Greece," and plenty of others. The biggest message I got was GAY IS GOOD! I gained so much confidence and started liking myself. I wanted to write this new discovery on walls!

I also got two penpals in February 1985 through a correspondence center at the same time I placed my book order. These friends gave me more information, support, encouragement, and praise. We still write each other and have developed a very strong bond.

Not long after I got the books, I had to deal directly with antigay violence and name-calling. The other kids had seen the title *Young, Gay and Proud!* on one of the books. The news went all over the home like wildfire. Before the week was out, I got teased, harassed, and got two black eyes.

The group home pressed assault and battery charges against the kid who gave me the black eyes. I had to testify in court against him. When he got up on the stand the judge asked him why he had hit me.

"Because he is a homosexual," he answered.

The judge responded, "Poor excuse for anybody. You need to learn how to control your temper. I sentence you to Barret Correctional Center, where they will teach you a thing or two. I authorize any length of time deemed necessary. Case closed."

I wrote my penpals to ask for their advice on how to handle the name-calling. They suggested three solutions: 1) ignore it, 2) stay away from the problem, and 3) say a creative phrase in return, such as, "Thank you for the compliment. Have a nice day, baby!" I didn't have a problem following the advice, but when I used the creative phrases some of the kids could not keep their cool. They cursed at me and threatened me, but they ended up getting restrictions.

In May 1985 my counselor friend got a new job and left the group home. We hugged each other for a long time – until I stopped crying – and I thanked her for all her support and guidance. She told me, "I helped you get a start. You are doing an excellent job. Now you must go seek your new friends and life. Take good care."

In November of that year I moved to a new group home. By that time my parents, the service agency, and the staff at the new home knew all about my gayness. The staff accepted me and were very supportive. My parents don't discuss it.

It wasn't long before word got out among the other kids that I was gay. The whole issue led to a group meeting where several people asked me if the rumors were true. I said, "Yes. I am gay and proud of it."

For a while I had to put up with a lot of name-calling and ignorance. I ignored most of it, but when it started to be an annoyance or when they hit me, I went to the staff. They were always very understanding and supportive, and usually gave the troublemakers a restriction or punishment of some sort. When the staff were not available, I used my creative phrases, like "You don't know what you are missing!" or "You ought to try it. It might be good for you." That really threw them.

After I turned sixteen, things began to cool out. I have had few, if any, problems with other residents bothering me. Some of the main troublemakers have been discharged from here, so those who continue picking on me have little support from anyone else. I have even had some kids come up and talk to me about my gayness. I talked to them honestly and openly, and I did not hesitate to answer their questions. Now, instead of picking fights, we go our separate ways. For me GAY IS GOOD!

Len Clumic*

San Diego, California

Welcome Nowhere

J*anuary, 1972:* "You should toy with the idea of studying law," my first therapist suggested.

"I like reading D.H. Lawrence," I answered.

"Try for a degree in history," he countered.

"But Walt Whitman is my idol."

"Be serious, Len," he said in all seriousness.

"I am. Tennessee Williams wrote six hours every day."

My therapist winced. *Len Clumic,* he must have thought, *a no good.*

I was a sophomore in college when my rehab counselor sent me to this square, who wore a goatee trying to be hip. It only succeeded in making him seem pretentious. I remember hoping his daughter, who stood framed in a family portrait on his desk, grew up to wear a moustache.

People were always trying to steer me in their direction. When I was seventeen, and still walking, another counselor wanted me to go to accounting school. My first sex partner accused me of running to tell the teacher because I didn't want him pawing me. I fled in one piece.

One person who didn't try to pressure me was Bob. He was a deejay who hosted this fantastic gay radio talk show. He filled me in on what being a gay male was all about. He and the other guests would talk the kind of talk that was to be found nowhere else.

I guess I loved Bob and the other men on the air. He was the closest thing I had to a role model and hero, if you can have a role model at the age of twenty-eight. When I first called in, I had been in my chariot for four years. This man had a sexy voice, and kept turning me on, even though I had no idea what he looked like. I never mentioned I was in a wheelchair, just that I was this shy guy living at home, and was I doing wrong by leaving my *After Dark* magazines where my mother could see them?

He said that was okay, and made me feel free as a bird. Then he said I should be ready to explain to her why I liked magazines with pictures of naked male ballet dancers if she asked. "Mom," I fancied myself saying, "I like the dancers because they are so free and beautiful; so alive and healthy in a way that I am not."

She never asked.

Bob was a great host, and he often did naughty things on the air which got him into trouble, like groping guests while interviewing them. This creative use of the airwaves did wonders for the scared who needed reassurance, the shy and reclusive, and the unenlightened who were buried alive under tons of heterosexual conditioning. Listening to Bob was like finding an oasis in the desert.

One day I convinced one of his guests to come up and give me a lesson in going all the way with someone — which I hadn't done until then. When I wanted a repeat visit, he told me to start a gay and handicapped group, which I felt smacked of segregation. I told him what he could do with his advice.

I was destined to meet a long line of snobs who were much too freaked out by my chair to see me as their equal. Even my first lover, my Devil, was just another variety of snob who treated the afflicted with a different attitude. These artificial types never seem to remember their outcast role in society, and will put me down for not being physically healthy like they are.

I am Len Clumic. When I was seven, my older sisters would entertain their girlfriends by throwing off their shoes to boogie woogie, hug each other, and giggle about boys they knew. They'd have pajama parties where they would look in the mirror and change their appearance with paint. My brothers would entertain their buddies like men, which meant sitting on the living room couch, with wide spaces in between, and listening to the Yankees hit home runs. Now shake my hand firm and buy a jalopy wid me to show da whole block who is king.

July, 1952: We lived in a neighborhood that by today's standards would probably be called a slum. Back then we just thought of it as a city block up in the Bronx. Our neighbors were mainly working-class Italian and Irish, and I was a part of them since my mother was Italian. My father was Czech. Since my affliction was some years off then, I wasn't caged in by four walls. I roamed the streets, parks, rooftops, empty lots, and fire escapes of my neighborhood. Living among a lot of lusty Italians, there was always excitement, plenty of music and laughter, plenty of celebrations.

And there were other kinds of excitement: the games, the gang battles, stealing and defacing property. Being in a gang meant that you were always trying to overpower a rival or impress another kid in your gang. We had lots of chances for close physical contact: a lot of wrestling with other boys. Since things were organized by age and size, you never had to worry about being at too great a disadvantage. The match ended when somebody cried "uncle," and I always delayed it to savor the warmth of the other boy's body, and the feel of his muscles gripping me.

What was more exciting about these activities was that no matter what, nobody ever squealed on anybody. So there was the possibility that you could pair off with a kid you liked, or had subdued once, or was a member of your gang, and go off together and do things. Since your kid was a "safe" kid, opportunities for sex came up.

There were gimmicks we would use to arouse one another, like talking dirty about girls. Another was to play out in the rain or snow so you would have to go into one of your houses and change into dry clothes. We would go down on one another, or jack off. You did this stuff anywhere. Maybe under a bed or in a closet, inside a cardboard box or in an empty lot in the tall grass.

You did this sort of thing until you were thirteen or so, then you got serious with girls and dropped your special pal. For those of us who didn't, there was the street corner society where you hung out being macho, until the opportunity for sex came and you could drop the act.

For me, this male bonding began to recede at age fourteen when I developed a disabling condition. I drifted into pornography — usually male physique magazines from Sweden or Germany — and relied on fantasies of the "old days" when Tony or Kevin invited you over to watch them lift weights, got you to feel their bulging biceps, and then got into hot and heavy sex.

"I'm new here. Is the music always this loud?"

"Sure, always," he coldly says.

"I really came to talk since I'm not in the right shape for dancing."

He makes no response, just gives me an embarrassed grin. So I move on. I hope the restroom is big enough for me.

"Ya really know how to whiz around in that thing. I have an aunt just like you," says a dude who is kind enough to pass my drink down to me.

"Yeah," I answer. Does he really think I'm like her?

"Yeah, she got one of them electric gizmos. Goes everywhere."

I smile and move away with my drink between my legs so it won't spill. I spot a dude giving me a glance and hope he's not doing it because I remind him of his uncle.

"You're nice," I say to a guy I think I might get somewhere with. "How about leaving together?"

"Love to . . . but I gotta be up at six in the morning."

I always meet people who have to be up early or have a bad cold or suddenly remember they're with someone after they've talked with me for an hour. I've got all their excuses categorized. I especially like the ones who have a lover they want to get back with, and so they're being careful:

"We don't have to let him know, just let it be a secret between you and me."

"Oh, but you don't understand," he says almost indignantly, "I made a promise to be faithful."

I sometimes tolerate a drunk or two, since it's better than

nothing. I wish I'd meet someone who'd just come out and say, "Sorry, I'd rather not."

May, 1973: Dear Mr. Clumic,

> I am sorry, but it appears our dating service doesn't have the facilities for someone with your special needs. Find your check to us in the enclosed envelope. I hope you will seek out opportunities in the ad section in which you saw us advertised.

The want ads? The nearest post office is twelve blocks away.

It's time for another therapist. This time he's gay.

"Patience," Dr. Lang says, "you've got to have patience, Len." We see each other every Wednesday. "I know you're depressed at not having a lover at the age of thirty-one; but while that may be crucial to your happiness and well-being, we must work on other areas such as self-esteem."

For six weeks, I listen to his meditation tapes. I listen at night and drift off to sleep hearing Dr. Lang's voice. I think I'm falling in love with him.

"Now that you're halfway through college, what are your plans when you graduate, Len?"

"I'd like to be a writer. I'm thinking of working for a publishing house where I could work my way up learning the book business."

"You've seen too many movies."

"I know, Doctor, but it's what I want. I feel I need to be in that world. I need that kind of stimulation."

"You know those jobs are very hard to find."

"Dr. Lang, I want to fix up my emotional life first."

"Yes," he mutters, "of course . . . and we must naturally see to that as well."

One day about a month later he's discussing *his* sex life with me: "We met in this posh restaurant and then went up to his place. The next day we went off to ski, and afterwards in his cabin, we screwed all night. In the morning he made delicious scrambled eggs for me and we showered together."

"Wow," I say, "all that from just eating in the right restaurant."

He laughs. He's in his shirtsleeves, and the sun is shining on him.

"Now, Len, we must get back to you."

"But, Doctor, I love hearing about your love life."

"I know; but that doesn't seem to help you, and that's what we're here for, after all."

I lean forward. "You're giving me glimpses into a world unknown to me, a world I only think of as fantasy."

"Living vicariously is not recommended treatment, Len."

I feel like puncturing his grave demeanor. "Why don't you ever have me lying down? I told you our first day that I can think better and am more relaxed lying down."

"That's old-fashioned."

"This office is too sterile, and your nurse too starchy."

He tries making more excuses. But I won't let him get out so easily: "I feel like coming here was a mistake. I feel I'm wasting my time . . . I'm in love with you."

He stops rocking in his chair. "I'm sorry about that." He ends the session. End of therapy.

July, 1975: I've been out of therapy for a year and have only six months left of college. In that year I've had mostly one-nighters or been used by men I didn't respect. I was slumming. My current roommate was a gay kid who needed a place until he found one of his own. He volunteered for the Switchboard, a gay clearing house, and one hot summer night he called me:

"Hey, Len, I have a guy here who needs a place for the night."

"What's he like, Vic?"

"He's twenty-three and has red hair. Born in Wisconsin and his name's Danny. I told him you were my roomie and all that."

"Okay, bring him back with you tonight."

Danny arrived needing a bath. He got one, plus a tuna sandwich — which he ate on my bed wearing only a towel. I never got a pick-up so easily, and never one who would need to spend the night. He was my first redhead. Chubby and kinda cute. He smiled shyly and we bedded down snugly together. I felt I could trust him, and I had no better prospects . . . but after a week he was weighing heavily on my finances and took off. He called a week later to say he had a guy I would like to meet. Being curious, and alone as usual, I gave in.

David was different from Danny, but equally poor. David came from Boston and loved the discos. Danny was his pimp, I gathered, but all he got was a meal and the floor to sleep on. This was too much for my roommate, and he moved out. Danny got his bed and David and I slept in mine. But Danny could see I wouldn't tolerate David for long, so two nights later he came home with the Devil himself. Rick Olson made an impression.

I can see ya need help, with no roommate and no steady."

"You talk so smooth and nice." *So handsome and blond,* I thought.

"I fuck nice, too."

He didn't have to sell me on it. Something clicked the moment he walked through the door. For ten months he stayed, and when it was all over he left a hole where my innocence had been, replacing it with a cynicism that would be permanent.

But Rick Olson, no matter what else he did, caused me to grow up. "Ya need to get out more," he said to me one bright morning. "Get up, lazy bones." He threw off the covers and we went out for what was to be the first of many long walks. I had never seen so much of New York as I saw that summer. All the people and places had a golden glow, as if a hidden power were emanating from them. For once I was part of the scene, and not just occupying a space. I wasn't lowering my eyes as I had been, not avoiding life like a cripple, but experiencing new streets, new vistas, new sensations. For the first time I entered a bar with someone the whole place knew was mine. I was in love! No longer huddled in the corner away from the action . . . I was *there.*

It ended when I found out he had been lying to me and cheating on me. I forgave him once, but it didn't stop. He left one night and only returned a week later to get his things. I didn't ask him to stay because if he had it would have been the death of my soul. No matter how twisted my body, I had to keep my soul unruined.

My friends said I had nothing to grieve over. Some even wondered why I knew him at all. But they couldn't know how he had touched me. Poor Rick; poor Len . . . neither of us in shape for winning the goal we had set out to win. My love's self-hate proved to be, for him, what my disability was for me: a crippling obstacle to his happiness and well-being.

I have this dream, where on one luminous day all the Lens and Ricks persecuted for their love will run through the sands of a golden beach, undespised and uncrippled. Above them is a brilliant blue sky, and before them the outstretched hands of the gods inviting them home to embrace and favor them.

Phillip Millhollin*

Council Bluffs, Iowa

Out of the Cocoon

When I was a kid, the word "gay" could always get a few giggles whenever my class would stumble upon it in a story or poem we happened to be studying. Of course, our teacher would always remind us of its older definition of "happiness," but being happy didn't seem to have anything to do with the meaning we had in mind.

Looking back, I see how we were victims of our parents' ignorance. To them the word "gay" stood for everything they didn't want in a son or daughter. The Church taught that homosexuality was unnatural and immoral, and my parents supported that view because they didn't know what being gay really meant. I grew up fearing the word, just as I did any other dirty word that threatened a mouth full of soap.

However, I now find that the word that would have insulted me at one time now makes me proud. Such new meaning comes in the realization of the fact that "gay" is a word that describes me, and it is my hope that in my life, homosexuality and happiness will not be totally unrelated, but will complement one another and lead people to a better understanding of me and others like me.

The realization of my homosexuality was a gradual one. As I ended seventh grade at the age of thirteen, puberty introduced me to the awakening of my sexual desires. As *I* became more aware of the pleasures that could come from sex, I began to find that my preferences were for other guys. I did not have any sexual relations with anyone, but I found that in masturbating, my fantasies centered on other guys and not on girls.

Although by the eighth grade I felt I had established my sexual preference, I still hadn't really accepted the idea that I was gay. I just didn't feel comfortable with the label, especially because of all the negative connotations it held for me at the time.

In junior high I was very shy and reserved. I had a low sense of self-esteem because I didn't see myself as popular or good-looking, and I couldn't see why anyone would want me as a friend. I didn't need another reason to look down on myself.

But in high school, my self-image gradually began to change. I began to come out of the shell I had built for protection, and I began to believe that some people might actually find me attractive as a friend. I became more open and outgoing, and found that when I was friendly to people, they didn't reject me.

While this enriched my life and gave me a heightened sense of self-worth, I still lacked the hope that any of my friends would accept the idea that I was gay. Inside, I continued to struggle to suppress my homosexuality, which conflicted with my desire to be honest with others. I became depressed that I had no one I could really open up to and who would be understanding and accepting. I don't know how I ever would have pulled myself out of such depths of despair if it were not for the Alyson Letter Exchange Program.

Until I discovered it, everything seemed hopeless, but I'll never forget the night I accidentally stumbled upon a radio talk show that just happened to be discussing homosexuality. I listened in awe to an actual discussion of this taboo subject on the air, and I frantically scribbled down the address of the pen pal service that they gave as a resource for young homosexuals who needed to open up to someone.

I immediately took their suggestion and obtained a P.O. Box;

then I sent off my first letter to the service. With it went all my elated hopes for contacting the person who could become the true friend that I had always wanted.

Unfortunately, my first correspondents didn't work out, but I was not about to let my hopes be dashed so soon, and I wrote off for another pen pal.

This time, my prayers were answered. I began a correspondence with Ken, from Michigan, who has since become one of my closest friends. He has given me all the understanding and acceptance that I could have ever hoped for.

We began writing in December 1985, when I was sixteen and he was almost eighteen. He had just come out to his parents, and they accepted him, a fact I found encouraging.

Over the next few months, he began to come out to some of his closer friends, and he found that those people who were his true friends still liked him and accepted his homosexuality as merely another facet of his personality. They were even *glad* that he had allowed them to understand him better by sharing this part of himself which they had not known before. This brightened my hope of someday finding friends who would accept my homosexuality, but I still wasn't quite ready to open up to any of my friends.

In the meantime, I came in contact with another guy through the letter exchange, but the relationship that developed between us became more than just a friendship.

His name was Michael, and he was a sophomore at a large, distant university in Iowa. From the first letter, I felt an attraction for him that was unlike any I had felt for another guy. He seemed to be everything I could have dreamed of in a lover. He was intelligent, very talented, and even handsome, and I was elated to find that he had an equally strong attraction for me.

I was overcome by the desire to meet him in person, and it was with great anticipation that I enrolled in a two-week summer music camp at the college he attended.

I couldn't believe I had really done it! I mean, there I was, someone who had once believed himself to be totally incapable of being loved, now preparing to meet someone who could become his first lover!

I was very nervous, and thoroughly horrified that he might

not like me at all upon seeing me in the flesh. My fears were put to rest when we met, for he expressed the deepest and sincerest friendship for me, something for which I was even less prepared than I was for rejection.

Even though I had made some good friends in high school, I had never known anyone who had a romantic interest in me. I guess I had lots of self-doubts about ever becoming involved in such a relationship, but as Michael and I spent more time together, I found our relationship leaning more and more towards a romantic one.

This was something that I had a lot of trouble accepting. I had developed such a strong fear of being rejected by anyone I cared a lot about that whenever I felt myself getting close to them, I would try to detach myself and hide my true feelings from them. I believed that if I didn't let people know I liked them a lot, I couldn't be disappointed by finding out that they didn't feel the same way about me.

But as Michael's love for me became more and more apparent, I began to realize what harm I was really causing both of us by being too afraid to show the love that I did indeed feel for him.

Gradually, I allowed myself to open up to him. I cannot fully put into words the great joy and happiness that I felt in the sharing of our mutual love for one another. It was the most tremendous feeling I had ever encountered in my life, and it is one I will never forget. Unfortunately, that feeling did not last long.

From the beginning, we had both been aware of our limited time together, but neither of us would admit that my last day at camp was fast approaching. When it did come, I expected a painful goodbye, but I had hoped that we could continue to write until the next time we could meet.

That didn't happen. On our last day together, Michael told me that he had decided he couldn't be gay for the rest of his life. The whole time we had been together, we had felt the pressure to be secretive about our relationship, which had put a lot of strain on our love for one another. This was a strain that Michael could not put up with. He felt that he could never really have a successful long-term relationship with another guy, and so he said he would rather look for finite relationships during college, and that he would eventually settle down and get married to a girl, like "everybody else."

What surprised me more than this was how calmly I accepted the situation. I knew that we had been put under some unnecessary stress by our attempt to keep our love hidden, but I believed that in the future we would have gradually found ourselves more comfortable in showing our love for one another, regardless of those around us. I wish he had given us a chance. I thought it would have been worth the wait.

My time with Michael has become a treasured memory. For even though our relationship failed, I was successful in overcoming my own insecurities and allowing myself to love, and to be loved.

That in itself is a greater joy than many people allow themselves in their entire lives, and I believe that I have just begun to live. At times, I do become depressed when I think about how difficult it is to make a gay relationship succeed, but I still have hope, and that's one word that will always serve as a promise that with the future will come change for the better.

About the Contributors

Jim Baxter is currently editor and publisher of *The Front Page*, a newspaper for gay men and lesbians in the Carolinas. He's been publishing since October 1979.

Wilton Beggs was born in a rural area of East Texas in the family farmhouse. "My grandparents were the children of Confederates," he says. "I didn't know 'damnyankee' could be two words until I went off to college; I've learned a lot since then." Still a Southerner, Wilton now lives in Dallas.

John J. Carr was born in Chicago in 1920. Since his thirty years of seafaring ended in 1975, John has earned his B.A. and two Master's degrees, as well as becoming very active in the San Francisco gay community.

Wayne Curtis is an editor and writer currently living in Boston. He is a native Virginian who holds degrees from the College of William and Mary and the University of Delaware.

Larry Duplechan is a writer living in Los Angeles. He has published numerous essays and stories, as well as two novels, *Eight Days a Week*, and *Blackbird*. His third novel, *Tangled Up in Blue,* will be published in early 1989.

Wayne A. Ferris was born in 1919 on the central plains of South Dakota. After retiring in 1981, he now spends his time writing, and doing volunteer work for several non-profit organizations in the Kansas City area.

Thomas Frasier has lived in several areas since leaving the Upper Peninsula of Michigan, including Indianapolis, north Georgia, central Tennessee, and Baltimore. He has written for the *Baltimore Gay Paper*, *Blueboy*, the *New Art Examiner*, and the *Advocate.* He has recently moved to Vermont with his life's companion to raise sheep, farm, and continue writing.

Vernon Maulsby is a poet and writer whose work has appeared in *Fag Rag, RFD, Philadelphia Poets, Gay Community News,* and in two chapbooks. He is currently working on another series of poems and a play.

Steve Nohava graduated from high school near the top of his class. Currently he is in the honors program at Old Dominion University, where he is maintaining a 3.76 GPA.

Lawrence W. O'Connor writes, "I am an extremely quiet, soft-spoken individual. Writing is my most powerful means of expression. It has provided me the opportunity to 'come out' from my closet of shyness."

Dan Restid is a thirty-six-year-old office worker who resides near Pittsburgh. Since leaving the Jehovah's Witnesses in 1981, he has been successful at reconciling his nature with his Christianity. This father of an eleven-year-old son has been out since 1985.

Scot Roskelley works in the public relations department of a Portland computer manufacturer and teaches college-level PR classes. Since writing his essay, Scot and his wife have concluded an amicable divorce. He is involved in a new relationship, and writes that he is "blissfully happy."

Don Sakers is a science-fiction writer and reviewer, and has written three novels, *Act Well Your Part, Lucky in Love* and *The Leaves of October*.

Gary M. Spahl has written ad copy and taught computer science to elementary school children. He currently manages public relations for a Boston non-profit organization working to build minority capacity in that city. "Ocean Park" is his first published piece, and is for Anne, with much love.

Laurence Wolf is a native of Manhattan who has lived in the Midwest for thirty years. A veteran of World War II and a grandfather, Larry came out at the age of fifty-nine, and has since been active in local gay politics.